Three-Speed
Dad in a
Ten-Speed
World

Three-Speed Dad in a Ten-Speed World

Kel Groseclose

BETHANY HOUSE PUBLISHERS
MINNEAPOLIS, MINNESOTA 55438
A Division of Bethany Fellowship, Inc.

Published by Bethany House Publishers
A Division of Bethany Fellowship, Inc.
6820 Auto Club Road, Minneapolis, Minnesota 55438

Printed in the United States of America

Library of Congress Cataloging in Publication Data

Groseclose, Kel, 1940-
    Three-speed dad in a ten-speed world.

    1. Fathers—Religious life. 2. Groseclose, Kel, 1940-
I. Title.
BV4529.G76   1983   248.8'421   83-2765
ISBN 0-87123-585-4 (pbk.)

Dedicated to my dad and mom, Bruce and Mildred Groseclose. Their patient, loving example taught me the meaning of parenthood at its best. Now as grandparents they are always supportive and never meddlesome.

ABOUT THE AUTHOR

KEL GROSECLOSE is Associate Pastor of the First United Methodist Church in Wenatchee, Washington. The son of a Methodist pastor, he grew up in the Pacific Northwest and Alaska, graduating from the University of Puget Sound, Tacoma, Washington, with a B.A. in psychology and sociology. He holds the Bachelor of Sacred Theology degree from Boston University and is presently enrolled in the Doctor of Ministry program at San Francisco Theological Seminary, San Anselmo, California. Kel and his wife Ellen are the parents of six children: teenagers John, Stephen, Amy; and juniors Michael, Sara and David.

PREFACE

Being a parent is an awesome responsibility. My particular specialty, fatherhood, demands qualities and skills far greater than I possess. I am often painfully aware of my need for more wisdom, strength and patience to do an adequate job of raising the six children our heavenly Father entrusted to this earthly father.

It is natural, as a preacher, that I choose a biblical text. The theme expressed in 2 Corinthians 3:5 offers me words of hope. "For there is nothing in us that allows us to claim that we are capable of doing this work. The capacity we have comes from God" (TEV). I readily confess my human incapacity and my dependence upon God in fulfilling the high calling of being a father.

This is a book the author "had" to write. It's a chance to brag; and the old saw that "confession is good for the soul" may be accurately applied.

I wish to acknowledge six unique persons who are essential to my endeavor. They provide me with enough raw material to fill volumes. I refer to those who address me as "Dad," "Hey, Pop," or "Whatsfordinnerdad?" I answer to them all.

I must also say a word about someone else. Even if you're not a whiz at math, you may have added one dad plus six children and arrived at seven. You get an "A" or a gold star. However, there are eight persons in this family if we count Mom. And believe me, she counts! She's not number eight in our household. She's number one! We couldn't have done it without her!

Kel Groseclose
Wenatchee, Washington
July 1982

TABLE OF CONTENTS

One

BUT NOBODY EVER TOLD ME

The reason God gives babies to young couples is not because they have enough energy (although they probably do). It's not because they can survive 3 a.m. feedings night after night (they likely can). It's not even because they're flexible and open to new ideas (they often are). No, the reason parenting is designed primarily for young couples is their lack of experience. They aren't fully aware of what lies ahead, so they don't know enough to be scared out of their wits.

If some prophetic soul had taken me aside before my wedding day and said, "You are going to be the parent of six children; for fifteen consecutive years you will have teenagers in your home; and it's going to cost you a bundle," I would have panicked and made a run for it.

But nobody ever told me what to expect, and I feel an obligation to reveal my on-the-job observations. My purpose is not to induce fear and trembling in the hearts of prospective parents. My hope, rather, is that some anxious or fatigued parent will stumble upon these words, laugh or cry, receive a shot of energy, and rediscover the joy of parenthood.

Nobody ever told me I would always have an audience. I do enjoy the approval and admiring glances of others. But the inquisitive eyes of small children are unique in their intensity and

11

ability to never blink. On Saturday mornings I go out to work on the car. I'm not much of a mechanic, but periodically I like the neighbors to think I know the difference between a spark plug and a tailpipe. I lean under the hood, trying to look knowledge-able as I poke around with my screwdriver. One child is squirming under my outstretched arms, another is balancing precariously on the bumper, and a third is jumping up and down by the fender. "Dad, what's that funny round thing with a hose sticking out?" I'm in luck, I know it's the air cleaner. But I dread questions of the "How does it work?" variety.

In springtime I grab my shovel and head to the garden spot. The handle is worn smooth from my enjoyment in turning the rich soil and breaking clods apart in preparation for planting. Worms of various lengths surface with each spadeful.

"Dad, look at that big worm! Can I have it?"

"Which worm?" I ask.

"The one that's about to wiggle inside your shoe."

My next word closely resembles Charlie Brown's famous ex-pression: "AAUGH!"

Dad must overcome any self-conscious tendencies when his audience is present. Like most audiences, they sometimes clap, they sometimes boo. Regardless of the reviews, this group will be back for the next show. And those moments can be wonderful teaching opportunities.

Nobody every told me how fast they would grow. I took eldest son, John (then fifteen), for new shoes. We sat and waited our turn. John removed his shoe. In a stage whisper no doubt heard throughout the shopping center, I said, "I thought I told you to change your socks!" He was wearing his most ancient pair with gaping holes.

"Relax, Dad, this is only the third day I've worn these. At least they match."

"Match what?" I muttered through clenched teeth. "The worn-out knees on your jeans? Your dirty fingernails?"

John placed his foot on the measuring device while the sales-person made the adjustments. "He needs an 11½."

"I'm afraid you've made a mistake," I advised her. "He's been wearing a size 9 which we bought only three or four months ago." I slipped off my shoe and placed my foot on the cold metal. (Whew! Socks with no holes.) It read 9½, the size I'd worn for twenty-five years. "John, put your foot there again. I'm sure she made an error—and quit stretching your foot."

"Dad, I couldn't stretch my foot even if I wanted to. Did it occur to you that I've *grown*?" It had crossed my mind. Kids are designed to grow; it's part of the system. I just didn't realize it could happen so fast.

Nobody ever told me that my wife and children would doze on nearly every car trip. As soon as we're out on the highway, heads start nodding and bodies begin reclining against doors. Nobody ever asks me if I'm willing to stay awake. They simply assume I'll remain alert. Whenever the vote was taken, I must have lost.

Nobody ever told me how hard it would be to find them when work needed to be done, and how impossible it would be to lose them when I wanted to be alone. If the lawn needs to be mowed or a pile of clean clothes awaits folding, try to locate a child. I can't figure out where they go. If by some misfortune they can't flee, they're primed with excuses. "Shucks, Dad, I'd like to help, but I've got a geometry test tomorrow. I've got to study right up till bedtime." I'm not a suspicious person, but when he's had all weekend to do homework, and he's now telling his sad tale with a baseball in one hand and a transistor radio in the other, I do wonder if I'm being conned.

Nobody ever told me that my children would know only two things to do with a door: leave it wide open or slam it shut. They leave it open when it's minus five degrees outside, or when the flies of August are circling the house, ready to dive bomb inside. They slam it shut when you're three steps behind and staggering beneath two heavy sacks of groceries.

Nobody ever told me they would borrow my stuff, with or without permission. Smeared on my chin after shaving is a blob of toothpaste which somebody wiped on my towel. They ask to borrow my favorite tie as they're dressing up for school crazy days! They scatter my tools all over the landscape. And now—the ultimate horror—they borrow the car.

Nobody ever warned me to be cautious in helping them select musical instruments. I wanted several of our children to play
the violin since I fiddle around some with old-time music. I had
forgotten how squeaky and shrill a violin can be in the hands of a
novice. If I might offer a little friendly advice: avoid all percussion
instruments. Happily, Amy's junior high band has eighteen sweet-
sounding flutes and only two drums. I thought we were safe when
I encouraged Michael to play the bass viol. It was so large, I assumed it would stay at school. Wrong. Every Tuesday morning I
lug this over-sized instrument to the music room. Every Friday, I
pack it home. I have yet to bump the bass on anything that may
damage it, but my shins have taken a beating—all for the privilege of having cultured children.

Nobody ever told me how "everyday" parenting can be. Actually, being a dad or mom is an every-minute affair, twenty-four
hours a day, seven days a week. Parents need to escape from
time to time, to go off by themselves for marriage enrichment.
But the best way to be renewed is right in the harness. Though
the constant demands of parenting get to me occasionally, the
unfailing flow of love from my kids does wonders for my soul.

Nobody ever told me a lot of facts. I probably wouldn't have
believed him if he'd tried. This way, my life is filled with surprises.
And each day I am surprised by joy and love.

*"Lo, children are an heritage of the Lord: and the fruit of the
womb is his reward. As arrows are in the hand of a mighty
man; so are children of the youth. Happy is the man that hath
his quiver full of them. . ."* (Ps. 127:3-5).

Two

NOT NOW, MY SON

It had been one of "those days," full of pressures at work, too much to do in the available time, and other assorted hassles. When I came home for dinner, five-year-old David was in the kitchen, sitting on a counter stool, pencil in hand, a library book beside him. "Whatcha' doin' there, Dave?" I asked.

"Writing a story," he replied. He was laboriously copying words with frequent pauses for erasures.

I read the evening newspaper and helped Ellen prepare the meal.

After dinner, David returned to his task. A commotion immediately ensued. "Who took my pencil?" he cried.

"That wasn't your pencil. It was mine. You stole it!" an older brother accused.

"Did not! I found it on the floor. It's mine!"

"Tough. Find yourself another one." He shed a few tears in the process of locating a new pencil.

"This one doesn't have a very good eraser," he gently complained. I glanced at his paper; the multitude of smears proved the accuracy of his statement. Another older brother (David is child number six, so everybody is older than he) passed through the kitchen, no doubt on his well-traveled route between the refrigerator and the television set.

"Hey! We just had dinner," I heard myself yell.

"But I'm hungry again, Dad." Could a thirteen-year-old's digestive system really work that quickly? The "refrigeraider" did, however, volunteer to find little brother a better pencil.

Mom was preparing to attend an evening meeting, so Dad drew cleanup duty. I'd spent all day doing what other people wanted.

By 7:30 I was ready to do what I wanted, which happened to be writing at my cozy desk in the sewing room. (One takes what space is available in a family the size of ours, and rejoices.) I retired to my corner, carefully shutting the door. I could still hear all the noises but not see what was happening. (I have a theory about child rearing: once I've heard the noise it's too late to do anything about it, so I relax and keep concentrating on whatever I was doing.)

Tap. Tap. Tap. The door opened a crack and a five-year-old hand clutching a crumpled piece of paper stuck itself into the room. A small, shy voice said, "Here, Dad, I did this for you." I managed to mumble a "Thank you, Dave," before asking him to please leave me alone.

"Shut the door on your way out. I'm trying to get some work done." Sigh. I set his paper aside and resumed typing. But the twenty-three erasures caught my eye. Then the first sentence leaped out at me:

Not now, my son.
It's getting late.

I continued to read:

I still have today
To ski and to skate.
Thank you, Dad,
For showing me how.
Give me my sled
And I'll belly flop now.

Inside my head the light bulbs flashed and the bells clanged. I thought, *What have I done? He's worked hours to give me a gift. And all I could do was grunt and tell him to get lost. Some loving father I am! The writing can wait.* I opened the door, entered the adjoining family room, lay down on the bean-bag chair, and David, Amy, Sara, Michael and Dad read David's library book. It was a clever Berenstein Bears story. However, I was not about to escape reading only one book. Five or six stories and fifty or sixty yawns later (I always yawn when I read bedtime stories), it was time for drinks and off to beddy-bye.

Then it was reflection time for Dad. *How many times,* I wondered, *do I say, "Not now, my son; not now, my daughter"?* There certainly were instances when that was a legitimate response. But not as often as I'd employed it. The phrase "not now" was usually followed rapidly by words of irritation or impatience, implying they should have known better than to ask at all.

I had a question-and-answer session with myself after this epiphany at my desk. I have numerous such discussions with myself—after all, who understands me better than I?

Question: Who cares if Dad is smart and has a large vocabulary?

Answer: Nobody but Dad.

Question: Who cares if Dad is kind and loving?

Answer: David, five other children, one wife and all my friends.

I'd been retaught this truth more times than I could count. It was up to me now to live it, to practice it day by day. If I'd really grasped it, I wouldn't have to be taught it again.

I still hold the right to close the sewing room door; I need time to be alone to create, to recuperate. Yet I need also to honor their need to open it, their claim to some of my time and energy. I have a theory (Before you complete this book you'll encounter many such theories.): There are critical moments in my relationships with my children when they may be devastated if I say, "Not now. . . ." They are at a turning point where my attention is crucial. There may be other instances when they simply shrug their shoulders and reply, "Okay, Dad, that's fine; how about tomorrow or next week?"

At those critical moments, only choice, quality time, not just "during-the-commercial" time, will do. I don't have much time to give in total hours, so the time I give them should be unhurried in their view, even though I know the multitude of things I have yet to do.

In basketball there's a type of defense called "one-on-one," different from a zone defense in which I guard a certain area around the goal. In "one-on-one" I stick to a specific person wherever he goes. It can be more tiring, especially if my assignment is to guard someone tall, quick and in top condition. In the father-child relationship, I can sometimes play a zone; I can perform my work in the world while I let Mom resolve most problems, answer difficult questions, and heal the hurts. But I cannot simply dump all these duties on her. It's not fair to her and it's not a good witness to the children. And I'm cheating myself. Dad's got to play "one-on-one."

"Not now, my son. Not now, my daughter." They'll accept that answer if they know I'll be there later. They need me. And I need them. I need them snuggled on my lap with my leg slowly going to sleep while I yawn sixty times. I need to receive their affection and love.

Someday, long years down the road, when I'm old and gray (make that older and grayer), suppose I have a problem. Suppose I'm lonely or ill, troubled, adjusting poorly to retirement, in grief. I approach my child, seeking understanding and support. What if he says what he learned from me: "Not now, Dad"?

"And the apostles, when they were returned, told (Jesus) all that they had done. And he took them, and went aside privately..." (Luke 9:10).

Three

SOMEDAY I MAY GROW UP

Someday I may grow up. But don't hold your breath. I haven't found the right season in which to accomplish this feat. Be honest. Is spring a time for maturing? I think not! Spring is for birth and buds, new life and tender shoots, delicate green leaves, and beans cracking through the soil. Spring is for digging in the garden, getting dirty fingernails and finding mud stuck on my shoes. It's for flying kites in gusty winds. It's for bringing out the bicycles, pumping up the tires, and hitting the road. It's for sore muscles, because this child's spirit is housed in a middle-aged body. Grow up in springtime? Never!

I'm not going to grow up during summer, either. That's my season to walk barefoot in the dewy evening grass and to run through a sprinkler on a hot afternoon, clothes and all. It's the season when my wife yells at me for getting grass stains on my best pants. It's the season for joy and exuberance: playing spontaneous ball games in the park across the street; chasing the dog around the yard for his bath; blowing dandelion seeds in the air while reciting, "She loves me. She loves me not"—and if the wind is blowing sufficiently, those dainty parachute seeds may glide all the way to the neighbor's lawn. Summer is no time at all for growing up. I might have to quit wiggling my toes in cold mountain streams or stop lying on my back to watch clouds silently fluff by as I imagine them to be a long-necked giraffe or a cat ready to pounce on an unsuspecting mouse. Precious time.

Of course, we mustn't forget summer's crowning activity—camping. It's best to try it first in the backyard. The tent didn't fall over at 3:00 a.m.? Somebody didn't get trapped inside a sleeping bag? Good, we're ready for the big time. Somehow I get everything packed in the car; there's no room left for people, but the gear is stowed away. I'm usually so tired by the time we're ready to depart that I want to cancel the whole event.

And when we return, the lawn is either brown and wilted, or a foot high; newspapers are yellowing on the steps (oops, forgot to call the paper girl); gasoline bills from the first day out are awaiting us; junk mail is bulging out of the mailbox; dirty dishes left in the sink have petrified; and the garbage I forgot to take out has ripened.

The kids are exhausted, too tired to help me unpack but not too weary to argue. "I got bit by the most mosquitoes."

"Big deal! I caught more frogs than you did."

"Well, I got lost. Nobody else did that, so there!"

"If it had been up to me, you'd still be lost, and I'd have your room and all your stuff."

We smell like stale campfire smoke, have a veritable mountain of dirty clothes, and are covered with assorted blisters, scatches, bites and plain old grime. "Dad, when can we go camping again? Maybe next weekend? We had a blast!"

If spring and summer are inappropriate seasons in which to mature, perhaps fall is the correct one. Wrong again! Fall is raking crimson and golden leaves into huge piles and then taking a flying leap. Fun! "It's my turn to be buried! Pile 'em on me!" Fall is harvest, with the joys of finding squash hidden under wandering vines and digging potatoes as though searching for treasure.

Fall is football in the front yard. The maple tree is one goal line and the spruce tree the other. The curb forms the first out-of-bounds and "watch out for the flower bed" forms the second. Even Howard Cosell would get tongue-tied trying to describe some of our games.

Fall is also jack-o'-lanterns to carve, caramel apples to get stuck in my mustache, a weird costume to don, and somebody asking, "Aren't you a little old for trick-or-treat?" Fall is traipsing across the road to the orchard and finding apples left in hard-to-get-to places. Those two or three apples peeking from the highest branches taste best of all.

And winter? By the process of elimination, that's when I must finally grow up. I protest once again. Winter is snowballs whizzing by my ear, an igloo caving in upon my head, a sled too small for my "mature" build, and a snowman with a carrot nose wearing that dress hat someone bought me years ago. I just couldn't wear that hat. Old men wear hats like that. Until I grow up, the snowman might as well do the honors.

And winter has that most special of all childhood events, Christmas. I intend to remain youthful through this favorite holiday. I want to keep a childlike sense of wonder as I enjoy the bright and colorful decorations, as I sing joyous carols, as I join the throngs in busy preparation, as I smell freshly baked cookies shaped like stars and camels. A child is equipped to experience the mystery, glory and amazement of Christmas, to be wide-eyed as he sees not only the heaps of gifts, but also as he observes the generosity of people.

If you should visit our home during the Christmas season, you'd probably find me sitting on the floor gazing at the manger scene, all the lights out except those on the tree. In the family room will be my old Lionel train. It was a Christmas present over thirty years ago, and it's become a tradition to bring it out every year at this time. Forbid that I should grow up at Christmas and miss its love and beauty and glow.

It appears that I shall pass directly from childhood to senility and detour around maturity. So be it. I ain't never goin' to grow up. You go right ahead. I'll keep scraping frosting from the bowl, licking the beaters, leaving telltale crumbs on the kitchen counter at night, enjoying puppies and kittens, and laughing at Road Runner cartoons.

Someday I may grow up. Read about it in my obituary.

"Verily I say unto you, Whosoever shall not receive the kingdom of God as a little child, he shall not enter therein" (Mark 10:15).

Four

IT COSTS HOW MUCH TO RAISE A CHILD?

A U.S. government study recently estimated that it costs between $61,000 and $68,000 to raise a child to age eighteen, depending upon the region in which the family resides. However, an article in a national magazine countered with the claim that these figures were far too low. By adding a ten percent inflation factor and increasing several obviously deficient amounts, the new total came to a whopping $252,111! Sixty-eight thousand seemed quite enough to me. I love my little rascals more than all the money in the world, but a quarter million seems a bit steep.

After I read those figures, it became clear that my family was in deep, deep financial trouble. I put a new battery in my calculator and set about computing the full extent of the bad news. If you decide to do this, I suggest you have a box of tissues handy.

Our six children had a combined total of 38 more years before the last one would leave the nest in 11 years. I then multiplied 38 by the cost per child per year: $536,446. Our annual cost would be a mere $48,768.

After I struggled back onto my chair, I attempted to approach the situation rationally. I wept. In that same eleven-year period, I projected earnings of approximately $350,000. That sounds like a lot of money, until one glances at the half-million-dollar figure above. Mom and I would be over $150,000 in the hole by the time we finished our child-rearing duties. I was no financial wizard, but I knew that breaking open piggy banks wouldn't quite cover the shortage.

I arrived at the following depressing conclusions:

(1) We could provide only two children with an all-expenses-paid life through age eighteen. The fairest method of selecting which two would be by granting scholarships. After applications were studied, the lucky winners would be announced at next Sunday's dinner.

(2) One child would be eligible for a work/study grant. Ten-year-old Michael had expressed a desire to drive an eighteen-wheeler cross-country.

(3) Two children would have to live off-campus and commute to home. We would provide free parking for tricycles and ten-speeds.

(4) Our youngest child—well, I really didn't know how to break the news to him. He would have to quit growing up by the end of the year. Perhaps after an older sibling left home, he could resume his progress toward eighteen. We would promise to review his case periodically.

Does it actually cost a quarter million dollars to raise a child? Not mine. The author of the article neglected a host of cost-efficient procedures. For example, our house features multiple-use bathrooms. Neither parent is likely to be alone there. One or more children join us at any hour of the day or night. While it's inconvenient, disconcerting, and sometimes embarrassing, fewer flushes mean a savings on the water bill.

We share bedrooms. Mom and Dad frequently share theirs with two dogs and several restless youngsters. With a regular double bed, it gets crowded. We've considered a king-sized bed but don't want to encourage the gatherings.

Our daughters save hot water by taking showers together. Their motive, however, is not water conservation but fear of being alone in the gloomy basement bathroom. A community bathtub policy also saves on hot water; we need only change toys from boats to dolls. It's time to drain and refill the tub only when the dirt begins to solidify into clumps of mud.

Our children make homemade greeting cards which are more creative than commercially printed ones. I delight in their scissors-and-glue gifts more than in plastic items purchased at a shopping center. It not only saves money, it keeps little fingers busy.

We spend less on vacations than the national average because our idea of an exciting time is modest. We crowd into our station wagon and head to Seattle, 150 miles west across the magnificent Cascade Mountains. You'd be amazed at what we do for next to nothing. We watch jets take off and land at the international airport. We ride the monorail to the site of the 1962 World's Fair. We stand on the docks and watch huge cranes unload containers from ocean-going freighters. We observe pleasure craft slowly advancing through the Lake Washington Locks into Puget Sound. We delight at the sight of enormous salmon leaping up a fish ladder. We wander through the zoo and other beautiful parks. Our rural kids get a thrill from riding an elevator to the top floor, or zipping up and down escalators. We look, touch, walk and become exhausted. We return home having spent little money but bringing back rich and happy memories.

The alarming figures were no doubt based on buying a new car every couple of years. Forget it. Even if I could afford one, I wouldn't want one. I am well aware of the great American dream of owning a new Japanese car. Though I don't wish to be unpatriotic, I intend to keep our old car as long as it's mechanically sound. I'm able to be relaxed with it; after all, what more can they do to it? The seats are already sticky from hamburger relish, ice-cream drippings, and globs of catsup. The exterior finish has been well-scratched at multiple levels by wagon tongues, tricycle handlebars and bike pedals. If we had a brand-new car, I'd be a nervous wreck. I'd probably park it a block away and walk home.

We also beat the "system" by practicing the ancient art of hand-me-downs. Our youngest children wouldn't recognize a new pair of jeans nor be comfortable with their stiffness. Their jeans come broken in, faded, with patches on the knees. If the zipper works and there are no holes too large to repair, it's a valuable garment, worthy of recycling. Kids grow so fast that it doesn't make sense to buy new clothes. We buy them their very own socks, shoes and underwear. The remainder of their wardrobe depends on what hand-me-downs we have in their size. They usually accept the practice gracefully and are sometimes even pleased, if they admired the former owner. Unfortunately, the system does begin to lose momentum in the teen years, when fashion-consciousness raises its expensive head. But we get twelve good years out of the method. It puts some strain on Mom, who is the official clothes sorter. When seasons change or school starts, I find her buried amidst piles of clothing. She has thus far always found her way back to civilization and sanity. We endure the effort by repeating, "Think of all the money we're saving."

Keeping our annual cost below $48,768 is a family affair. We roofed our house together. We grow a small but productive garden each summer. We repaint a lot of used furniture.

But raising children can never be calculated in mere dollars. The cost is infinitely greater. Who knows what it takes to go days without sleep when a child is sick? Mom and Dad know. Who can calculate the depreciation on parents' bodies and souls? Who can apply a dollar figure to hours of supplication and prayer? Who can appraise the value of volunteer work as schoolroom mother, Cub Scout leader, or Sunday school teacher?

Money is the least of my concerns. It comes in handy, but it cannot cover expenses like emotional energy and undying devotion. Though I spend more money than the national average on these items, and have not love, I am a poor father. I am called to love them extravagantly, share my time liberally, and laugh or cry freely.

While I'm on my parental soapbox, permit me one additional observation. The compiler of national averages did not mention the dividends. I am rich indeed with slobbery kisses; hugs and squeezes from dirty hands; the echoing of happy voices through the house; eyes that twinkle with joy; and heartfelt statements like, "Dad, I love you heaps and loads!"

Forty-eight thousand a year? Sixty-eight thousand per child? A quarter of a million dollars? I'm not impressed. Scared, but not impressed.

"And he said unto his disciples, Therefore I say unto you, Take no thought for your life, what ye shall eat; neither for the body, what ye shall put on. The life is more than meat, and the body is more than raiment. For all these things do the nations of the world seel: after: and your Father knoweth that ye have need of these things. But rather seek ye the kingdom of God; and all these things shall be added unto you" (Luke 12:22-23, 30-31).

Five

EVERY DAD OUGHT TO HAVE A TREE HOUSE

We moved into our new home during midwinter. The yard lay buried under two feet of snow and the sidewalks gleamed with treacherous ice. Cherry and apple trees in the orchard across the street looked like a jumble of huge twigs. At the far corner of our lot stood a small tree, about 15 feet tall. I could tell it was a maple because a few tenacious seedpods and brown leaves still twisted and bobbed in the cold wind.

We spent so much time and energy moving in—cleaning, painting, decorating, and basking in the happiness of owning our first home—that we hardly noticed winter slipping away and spring making her first tentative gestures. I found a garden spot beside the carport by stepping ankle deep in mud which had just thawed. Crocus and daffodil shoots peeked shyly through the cluttered flower beds. As the snow disappeared I observed that no one had raked leaves in the fall. The grass was covered with a dark, partially decayed matting. I had an instant compost pile. And the little maple tree burst forth into life. Buds swelled and broke open, revealing a delicate green.

"Dad, can we have a tree house? Please?" The request was voiced and voiced until I thought I had an echo inside my eardrum.

"Kids, it's not a very big tree. We'll have to build something

31

fairly small." We found some old lumber piled by the back fence—not much to look at, but solid and usable. We extracted all the bent, rusty nails as we arranged our valuable find. Then we entered the architectural stage. We studied the maple from every possible angle. We sketched ideas, mine being simple and theirs complex. "No, you cannot have a two-story, three-room tree house," I said. "How about a platform with a railing around it?"

We purchased a supply of box nails at the hardware store, gathered the necessary tools and borrowed a twelve-foot ladder from the orchard owner. I climbed up and balanced precariously on the limbs while John and Steve handed up two-by-fours. "No, not that one. I need the long board over there." The boys learned sawing and hammering. Dad learned patience.

Slowly the frame took shape. We had to make frequent adjustments to the unique configuration of branches. We were finally ready to nail down the flooring. As soon as three or four boards were in place, everybody wanted to come up and stand. Even Mom gingerly ascended and kindly said, "My, this is nice." She made a rapid descent. One after the other, kids trekked up the ladder, stood on the platform a moment, stuck their heads through the leaves and uttered squeals of delight. The "open house" slowed construction a bit, but it was good to know our efforts were appreciated.

We anchored three steps to the trunk, far enough apart so kids younger than four or five would be unable to climb up. I didn't want to worry more than I already did about someone falling out. I continued to veto all of John's grandiose schemes for trapdoors and rope ladders.

The tree platform became a place of their own, a retreat where the kids might be alone, away from the prying eyes of adults. It served to release their powers of imagination: it was a fort under attack by desperadoes; a B-52 pursued by fighter planes; a castle high on a mountain; a doll house for Amy and Sara's substantial collection. On warm summer days, it doubled as a lunchroom. Mom packed lunches and Dad handed everything up to their outstretched hands. Somebody always spilled juice. Bread crusts and potato chip crumbs dotted the grass beneath. Conveniently, the dogs and the birds provided volunteer cleanup crews.

During the next several years, my children reminded me often that we had a platform, not a genuine tree house. "Houses have walls and a roof, Dad. All we've got is a floor." Then a colleague at work offered us a stack of used plywood paneling. The platform was soon transformed into a cozy house. And we had just finished reroofing our house, so leftover shingles protected the aerie from the deluge of rain and snow. Carpet scraps formed a colorful floor covering. Now they had a bona-fide tree house.

This was all accomplished in midsummer, while the maple leaves were large and lush, completely camouflaging the structure. After a particularly frosty autumn night, however, I glanced out the living room window. The maple had shed most of its leaves. "Where did *that* come from?" I asked with shock and dismay. Our tree house loomed in the bare branches exposed for all the world to see. Every carpentry error glared forth. It looked like a giant Snoopy dog ready to pounce vulture-style on innocent passers-by. I counseled myself to be strong. The neighbors were certain to express their opinions with either laughter or anger. I began to pray for an early spring and for gigantic leaves. (But it has proved handy in directing persons to our home—"Drive down Brown Street until you see a funny-shaped tree house bigger than the tree.")

I've discovered the tree house is a great place for Dad, as well as for the kids. There's no telephone or doorbell, only the gentle rustle of leaves and the cool, silent shadows. I relax as the tree sways in the summer breezes with a rocking chair effect. I rest above the cares and trials of the moment to daydream just as the kids do: I'm in a rustic cabin hundreds of miles away in the wilderness; I'm in a sailboat in the crystal waters of the Caribbean. The tree house is a means of good, healthy escape, better than a television adventure series or a score of cheap novels.

This house among the leaves also provides a quiet chapel, where I can think about God and talk to Him. Only honey bees straying from the neighbor's apple blossoms interrupt my reverie—and kids who want their tree house back. "Come on down,

Dad. Our secret club is ready to meet." My most frequent inter-ruption is wife, Ellen, as she hollers from the front door, "Kel, you're wanted on the telephone!" So I grudgingly return to the world of responsibilities and salaries, of interest rates and shirts with ties. I'm not certain which is the real world, the peaceful one among the leaves or the frenetic one awaiting my attention on the ground. Perhaps both are essential.

Anyway, I'm glad we built a tree house. It's a special place for our children, for the neighborhood kids, and for Dad. I think every dad ought to have a tree house, don't you?

"And when he had sent the multitudes away, he went up into a mountain apart to pray: and when the evening was come, he was there alone" (Matt. 14:23).

Six

I LOST MY COOL AND DON'T KNOW WHERE TO FIND IT

My wife, their mom, was sick. I was weary and discouraged. Fatigue and a bad mood were an unproductive duo: they egged each other on. With Mom feeling poorly, Dad had to do double duty. I'd had enough trouble doing single duty. She had a bad head cold and hopefully, with a few days rest, she'd be back in the harness. The way I was handling it right then, however, that few days might as well have been several decades.

The day had not started gracefully. I had gotten less sleep than I felt entitled to, so I was not overjoyed when morning unveiled its bright self. The digital clock glowed incessantly, the seconds moving so quickly they blurred in my squinty eyes. Noise began to filter up from the lower regions of the house. The sound of running water persisted. *How long does that kid stay in the shower?* I thought. *He takes one every day. He can't be that dirty.* Soon came the high-pitched whirr of his hair dryer. Bedroom doors opened and closed, dogs whined to be let outside, and toilets gurgled as they repeatedly flushed and refilled. I just wanted a few more minutes buried under the soft, warm covers. Was that asking too much?

After rising, I waited my turn for the bathroom. "Who's in there?" I mumbled rather urgently, my voice low-pitched and gravelly.

"Me, Dad," a shrill, small voice replied. My ears could not yet discriminate sounds well enough to determine which child had spoken. It really didn't matter, the room was occupied. Well, the milk needed to be brought in from the front porch; the curtains needed opening; the coffee and cocoa water needed turning on; and the cat was meowing and scratching at the kitchen window screen, causing involuntary shivers in my back muscles. I fulfilled those duties, then hustled upstairs again just in time to see another little person close and lock the bathroom door. Click! "How long are you going to be in there?"

"Dad, I just got in here!"

Back I shuffled to the kitchen and got down the cereal boxes and arranged the puffs, flakes, crunches, loops and O's. Steve came up the stairs, hair perfectly coiffed, teenage body squeaky clean. It wasn't his fault he was thirteen. So I accepted the justice of being the parent of a thirteen-year-old son; after all, I had put my parents through a similar trauma. Nevertheless, I felt myself tensing as I heard his ever-growing feet tramping my way. (I anticipate trouble before it occurs, no doubt creating a climate conducive to trouble.)

Each child had a designated spot at the breakfast counter. It had taken years to observe eating habits and personality types so we could make seating assignments. The tidy eaters sat around the corner from the sloppy ones. The child who had to spread out his elbows like a giant bird preparing for flight sat at the very end. It was all very scientific. So guess where Steve sat. On his designated stool?—Does gooey bubble gum stay out of children's hair? Do seven-year-olds remain clean when they're ready to go someplace important?—No way. No way. And no way. I struggled to keep my emotions under control. My coping energy was fading fast. I just wouldn't notice him. He'd be catching the school bus in fifteen minutes. Surely I could stand it that long.

"S-l-ur-r-rp!" Oh, no! He was slurping his Wheaties. I could understand slurping hot soup, or tea which had spilled in a saucer, but cold cereal at 7:00 a.m.? By a thirteen-year-old sitting in the wrong place? When I hadn't been granted my bathroom privileges yet? I confess, I lost my cool. The gravelly tone in my voice suddenly departed and I yelled, venting my irritation. *Funk and Wagnalls* defines irritation as "being easily annoyed." A lot they know. I am not easily annoyed. I might be convicted of justifiable irritation, but even Perry Mason could never make "easy annoyance" stick.

Once I'd blown up, my problem was how to recover. When I'd lost my cool, I didn't always know where to find it. After surgery the patient is wheeled to the recovery room where nurses hover round, attending every need, monitoring vital signs. It's the epitome of sympathy and compassion. But what did I get when I was upset and needed soothing? Mostly dirty looks. I had to recover on the job, receiving no special attention, not even the use of the bathroom.

So I kept toiling. At least the next breakfast shift wouldn't slurp cereal. They would just leave toast crusts and donut crumbs lying about, let the dogs lick raspberry jelly from their fingers, spill a box of cereal (a full one, of course), drip cocoa on light-colored shirts, and chop the margarine stick into a hideous blob.

I was exhausted by the time the last two skipped merrily off to school. Praise God for teachers! "My turn! It's my turn!" I exclaimed as I danced down the hall to the bathroom.

I made my escape to my office. I think my secretary wondered why I was getting so little done. I decided against attempting an explanation. There wasn't time to do an adequate job. I returned home at noon to check on how Ellen was feeling, and hoping for a peaceful lunch. It was not to be. The morning's mail brought a publisher's rejection slip for the best piece I'd ever written. Why couldn't anyone but I, my family, and my circle of friends perceive my writing skills?

When school was out I headed home again to greet the children. I listened to tales of woe and boasts of successes. I cut and quartered some Red Delicious apples, and set out crackers and cheese slices, feeling very much the competent father. "I'm still hungry, Dad" popped my bubble.

"You're supposed to be," I retorted. "This is only a snack, not a seven-course banquet."

Dinner was a cacophony rather than a symphony. "I want"

and "give me" prevailed by a large margin over "please" and "thank you." Michael remained sitting at the table because he didn't appreciate my creation, a hamburger-rice casserole. He sat there, alternately glowering at me and showing revulsion toward his plate. I cleaned the kitchen, stuffed dirty clothes in the hamper, and readied the younger children for bed. Our two teenage sons seemed more self-centered than usual. "Take me to activity night, Dad." He didn't ask if I could or if it would be convenient; he issued a demand. I thought I deserved a request, a polite one at that.

"I've got to have an advance on my allowance," pleaded our eldest.

"Son, you just got your allowance last week. Remember? You still have three weeks to go. What did you blow it on this time?"

"Oh, Dad, you don't understand! Stuff costs more than when you were a kid—a whole lot more. Haven't you heard of inflation?" I drove Steve to school-activity night. I tucked the little ones into bed. I robbed my piggy bank to advance John a couple of dollars. I picked Steve up. I had planned to settle into my easy chair and watch a football game on television. I was now able to understand Michael's glowering better. Several times during the day I thought I'd found my cool and I was finally beginning to relax and calm down. But whenever I was about to reclaim it, something had intruded to send my cool fleeing once more.

The reality of being a father is that I am apt to lose my cool every now and then. I'm growing in patience, but until the job's done, I'd best perfect the art of finding it again as quickly as possible. It usually hasn't strayed far. One of the children might return it to me wrapped in a kind word or a spontaneous hug. My wife might fix my favorite dish for dinner, making me feel loved and significant. An emotional movie on television might bring moisture to the corners of my eyes and mellowness to my soul.

The important thing for me is to keep searching, never to despair. Somebody will find my cool. I might even trip over it on my way to kiss the kids good-night.

I have a parental principle I seek to follow: don't go to bed until you've found your cool, until you've resolved any conflicts and released any tensions. If I go to sleep in peace and harmony, the next day has a chance of bringing me joy. I may even be able to smile while a certain son slurps his cereal.

"Be ye angry, and sin not: let not the sun go down upon your wrath" (Eph. 4:26).

Seven

I'M A THREE-SPEED DAD IN A TEN-SPEED WORLD

I should have known better than to join a race down Brown Street on my elderly three-speed. (Actually, the second gear doesn't work, so it's a three-speed minus one.) I allowed myself to be suckered in. "Aw, come on, Dad, we'll take it easy. We'll watch out for you." I could freely admit I was past forty, but forty was not synonymous with decrepit. The old man still had power in his legs. I'd show those whippersnappers!

The starting line was at Brown and Springwater. We assembled, circling and milling until the last competitor arrived. My two teenage sons looked smug and confident on their racy ten speeds. Fourteen-year-old Jimmy from across the street was revving up his BMX, complete with mag wheels. An entourage of younger neigborhood children were poised on their clever bikes with bright streamers, reflectors and fancy handle grips. The excitement of a showdown was heavy in the Saturday afternoon air.

I felt out of place, not because I was almost three times older than anybody else, but because I felt bad for my old bicycle. It has no complex gear system; just a small metallic box with a lever that goes "click-click." The handlebars don't sweep under in elegant fashion; instead, they stick out awkwardly, exposed to the barely-disguised sneers of the adolescent set. My bike is not passsionate

41

purple with gold stars and stripes. it is basic black, accented by rust spots.

We jockeyed for position, first one tire then another creeping ahead to gain a slight advantage. "Everybody get your front tire behind the crack in the asphalt," I hollered, "or the race is off." We had neglected to select a starter. Who could we find to yell, "On your mark. Get set. GO!"? We picked four-year-old David, the only one who couldn't ride a bike, hoping he could remember the order of words long enough to get us going. "Okay, Dave, no cars are coming. Say it now!"

"On your mark. Get set. GO!"

We sped down the street. I kept my body low to minimize wind resistance, since I was obviously the one racer most susceptible to that problem. We were to go two blocks to the corner in front of our house, and turn at the manhole cover in the middle of the intersection. It seemed simple enough, except that son John interpreted the guidelines to mean he should turn in *front* of the cover, and I thought it meant to go all the way *around* it. We were neck and neck. Well, maybe he was slightly ahead; because when he tried to turn across my path, I heard a noise like the clattering of a stick along a picket fence. His foot pedal had ripped half the spokes from my front wheel. It was a sad moment. I wasn't angry. I was in grief. My beloved bike was hurt. His sassy ten-speed had nary a scratch. "I'm sorry, Dad. You really shouldn't try stuff like this with your old bike."

"What do you mean? I had you right where I wanted you. I would have taken you on the straightaway."

Ellen, dear supportive wife that she is, came running to the scene of the commotion and added, "Serves you right, acting like this at your age!" My ego received more of a beating than my bicycle had. It's tough being a three-speed dad in a ten-speed world.

The world has speeded up since I was a child. There's been an incredible knowledge explosion, particularly in the fields of science and electronics. Temptations are more numerous and far more enticingly packaged. A smorgasbord of entertainment options entices our children and youth.

It's no wonder I frequently hear my elders bemoaning the terrible state of affairs. "You certainly have my sympathy trying to raise children today," they say, while slowly shaking their heads. I don't need their sympathy, but I could use a word of encouragement. Their usual parting comment is, "I'm sure glad we don't have kids at home anymore." With such a negative attitude, I'm thankful they've completed parenting too. However, our kids still reside in the nest, and we're trying our best to cope with the financial pressures, the educational demands, and a multitude of other daily stresses. We're attempting to keep it all together: to find the correct change for school lunches two minutes before the bus arrives; to make the beds before it's time to climb in again; to locate spoons and bowls for breakfast when we forgot to run the dishwasher last night.

Knowing that children do grow up, that parents have succeeded in past generations, inspires me. Perhaps pressures are greater today. Perhaps divisive influences are more intense. I'm not going to knuckle under. I deeply desire to succeed as a parent, not only for my sake but also for theirs.

When I have completed my fatherly tour of active duty, I hope to do more than sigh with relief. I don't want to say, "Whew! We made it." I want to rejoice in the intimate relationships we built, in the love we shared, in the tears we shed, in the giggling and laughter, in the sacrifices and blessings. How about a loud, "Hallelujah!" instead of a whimper? I know I shall not be physically or emotionally capable of a second go-around. Yet, I hope to be *willing* to do so, to be able to say with conviction, "That was quite an experience! We made a lot of mistakes, but I wouldn't trade it for anything."

It requires effort for me to survive and triumph in this ten-speed world. My pre-space age body is not designed to conform to the shape of a ten-speed bicycle. I'm accustomed to balloon tires, coaster brakes and a wide, triangular seat. I have great difficulty balancing on skinny tires, shifting all those gears, and perching on that hard, narrow contraption that passes for a seat. I also grumble and make ugly faces when attempting to repair those complex machines. I was able to take my bike completely apart and reassemble it when I was twelve years old. And I enjoy tinkering on my three-speed minus one—maybe some day I'll even fix the "minus one." But adjusting brakes or removing the rear wheel on a ten-speed induces tremors of fear. Don't give up on this old guy, though. I'm learning.

I receive periodical reminders of my ancient origins. I was helping one of our grade-school children with an American history lesson. I am not an expert by any means, but the subject interests me and I have retained a fair number of facts amid the cobwebs. We were discussing the Civil War when he looked at me with wide eyes and asked, "Dad, how do you know so much? Were you a friend of Abraham Lincoln or something?" I had been feeling quite young and frisky till then. Am I that far out of touch with the trends, fashions and innovations they take for granted?

I admit that I cannot compete with them in electronic games. I am not to blame, however. The auto racing, baseball, Ping-Pong and space games were not invented until after my reflexes had started their journey down the back side of the mountain. And I really don't mind "being over the hill," as they say. There are some wonderful things on this side I never noticed when I was laboring up the steep slopes.

I'm a three-speed dad in a ten-speed world, and proud of it. Who needs all those other gears? What's the rush? My kids won't ride my three-speed and I can't ride their ten-speeds. What I can do is help them choose their destinations as they travel along. Then I'd better pull over to the side of the road so I won't get run over. Again.

"Only take heed to thyself, and keep thy soul diligently, lest thou forget the things which thine eyes have seen, and lest they depart from thy heart all the days of thy life: but teach them thy sons, and thy sons' sons" (Deut. 4:9).

Eight

DAD'S WILLING TO BE A FOOL

I think I look pretty sharp in my navy blue three-piece suit, especially with the reversible vest turned to the houndstooth pattern. My shoes really dazzle 'em with the spit-shine I learned in the Air Force ROTC. And when I have my hair combed and mustache neatly trimmed, I cut a fairly impressive figure, though in all humility I do not claim to be distinguished looking. People probably glance my way and silently muse, "Now there's a semi-handsome man."

I have a theory about clothing for dads: if the item has a problem that you can hide, don't hesitate to wear it. A good outward image can be created with shabby clothes if you use ingenuity. Well-polished shoes allay any suspicion about the gaping holes in your socks. A vest handily camouflages spaghetti stains on a tie, but the classic illustration of this technique is underwear. Mine are dotted with paint and sagging with terminal stretch marks—and nobody knows. Sure, I worry about having an auto accident and being carted to the hospital; may I remain unconscious until garbed in an institutional gown. Yet in spite of all these secret defects, I can be downright dashing on occasion.

Then I arrive home. I've already received the approval, and even the praise, of the big world out there. I've been treated as a somebody, a man of stature, substance, clout. After all, I bring home the bacon. (Truthfully, I bring home more cheap hamburger and hotdogs than bacon.) I step from my car with style and grace. So how am I greeted? Dogs with muddy paws jump at my creased pants. Kids with sticky hands hug my legs. Mom with her flour-dusted apron cuddles close. I flee to the bedroom closet to become a reverse Superman. Off go the fancy duds and on come my jeans, tattered sweat shirt, and well-traveled sneakers.

At work, people listen to my words with deference, at times calling my advice wisdom. While I may not command attention like E. F. Hutton does, I am accorded a measure of respect. Can this be the same man who hunkers down on the floor and chases a four-year-old around the room on hands and knees, making sounds like "gitchie-gitchie goo"?

The snazzy suit and the slightly swelled head must both be checked at the door when entering the microcosm called home. The kids won't tolerate my delusions of grandeur. They hurl reality into my consciousness with a thud. "Hey, Dad! Where'd you shave this morning? At the blood bank?"

I learned early that, as a parent, I must be willing to be a fool. I don't mean dumb or slow of wit; a dad's got to be clever and able to be one jump ahead of them. A fool is variously defined as a mental defective, a dolt, or simpleminded person. This latter definition is closest to my meaning here. As a fool, complex thought is less helpful than simple love and clear purpose. Eloquence takes a backseat to frankness. Handsome finishes way behind functional. I'm quite willing to be thought a simpleminded fool if it refers to my ability to be playful, to not worry what others may think of my behavior.

I'm frequently a fool at work, but it's usually unintentional. At home I act that way on purpose. How else can I explain why I go with the kids to Saturday matinees? I duck flying popcorn, get a crick in my neck from sitting in the front row, and discover my shoe is glued to the floor by a massive wad of bubble gum. Being a fool allows me to carry a two-year-old upon my shoulders while he drools on my head and uses my ears for handles. It makes me willing to eat jelly beans held far too long in a sweaty palm— "Daddy, I saved this purple one just for you."

Since this dad is a fool, I am qualified to:

• Play hide-and-seek and peek-a-boo behind the furniture.

- Drive Tonka trucks for sandbox construction projects.
- Kiss "ouchies" to make them well.
- Move my mouth in funny contortions when spoon feeding a baby.
- Conduct funerals for dead hamsters and parakeets.

I'm at my foolish best during bath times. I've devised a number of diversionary tactics to make baths in general, and hair washing in particular, a delight rather than a life or death struggle. I scoop a load of water in a small plastic bucket and make airplane sounds as I suspend it over their heads. They scramble for a washcloth to cover their eyes as I proceed on my bombing run. Splash! It's amazing. When I wash hair by the usual method, I hear all kinds of cries and complaints, but when I B-29 them, I dump twice as much water with hardly any whimpers.

Variety is essential. They soon tire of one approach, so I've added others to my repertoire:

"Hurricane," complete with whistling wind, crashing thunder, and a great downpour of rain;

"Tidal wave," in which I envision a mighty wall of water coming closer, closer, closer;

"Submarine," in which I yell, "Dive! Dive!" while rinsing. Yes, it's a grown man, supposedly mature, kneeling beside the tub, wetter than the naked little bodies in it, and making all sorts of strange noises. It certainly helps if Dad's willing to be a fool.

I consider myself to be sane and of sound mind. I just think being a fool is a very wholesome occupation, not only on April first or in the privacy of home, but at anytime everywhere. I'd like to pack my three-piece suit in plastic wrap, place it high in a remote storage closet, slip on my faded blue denims, and be plain, unadorned me—holey socks, paint-speckled T-shirt and all.

St. Paul wasn't a father. But he understood and wrote, "We are fools for Christ's sake" (1 Cor. 4:10). So let's hear it for foolish Christian fathers!

"But God hath chosen the foolish things of the world to confound the wise;... that no flesh should glory in his presence" (1 Cor. 1:27, 29).

Nine

GLORIOUS INTERRUPTIONS

We had just gathered our family around the dinner table. I had turned off the TV and towed Michael away from the Atari. The meal looked delicious and I was hungry. At the precise moment between grace and my first bite, the telephone rang. I'm certain a telephone rings more loudly at mealtime and in the middle of the night than at any other time.

I had no more than lifted the receiver when the doorbell rang. Ellen went to answer it, leaving six children and no adult at the table. What happened next could be the theme for a book entitled "Lord of the Flies Rides Again." The six immediately reverted to jungle etiquette in the absence of an authority figure.

Sara spilled her milk while reaching for the catsup which Stephen refused to pass. Michael fed the dogs his serving of cauliflower. (The dogs believe anything handed from the table must be good.) Amy sneaked into the kitchen to pour her glass of milk down the drain and refill it with juice. John crammed his mouth with food, grabbed an extra handful of carrot sticks, and went back to watch television. Stephen yelled at John to sit down and then helped himself to dessert. In his hurry not to be caught he bumped into Amy, causing her juice to spill. The dogs were almost delirious trying to lick fast enough to keep pace with the disasters.

Neither the phone call nor the visit required more than a few minutes, but that was enough. Cleaning the dining room and restoring order required the rest of the evening.

After an experience like that, one may question the validity of putting "glorious" and "interruptions" in the same book, let alone side-by-side. An interruption is usually a nuisance. Yet, I have discovered that an interruption can halt the treadmill of monotony and set the stage for a serendipitous event. But it's up to me whether it has creative and glorious results or ends in calamity.

It was Friday, my day off. I had it all planned. After doing some long avoided yard work, I was going to take Ellen to lunch. Then the phone rang. "This is Hazel at Lewis and Clark School. We have one of your children lying on a cot in the sickroom."

"Who is it this time?" I asked.

"Sara."

"What seems to be her problem?"

"I really don't know. She looks kind of white."

"Well," I answered, "she *is* Caucasian."

"No, no, she's very pale."

"Oh, all right. I'll come and get her."

Once home, Sara appeared to be only slightly upset, showing rather vague symptoms. But there went my well-planned afternoon. Mom, Dad and Sara sat down to eat around our L-shaped kitchen counter. We enjoyed sandwiches from Sara's sack lunch as we visited.

That morning, in each school lunch, Mom had packed a chocolate-covered marshmallow bunny. Sara's eyes lighted up when she discovered the bunny tucked in a corner of her sack. She carefully removed the wrapper, broke the candy into three pieces, and offered Mom and me the two larger ones. My first impulse was to refuse her gift, for my children frequently give me bread crusts, half-eaten apples, melted Jell-O, and other prizes of dubious value. But part of a chocolate bunny—now that was a gift from the heart! Yes, Sara had interrupted our plans. She had also brought us an unscheduled blessing.

When Mount St. Helens blew its top in May, 1980, we experienced a dramatic interruption. Sunday had dawned in splendor. I had heard the thunderous eruption almost a half hour after the actual explosion, but assumed it to be a mighty sonic boom. We did not hear the news until after church. By noon the sky had an eerie gray cast, and the fine ash particles set my teeth on edge.

Son Stephen devoured his lunch, hopped on his new ten-speed, and headed for a friend's house. Soon the dust was swirling and the pungent smell of sulphur irritated my nose. Though it was early afternoon, the sky grew ever darker and more ominous.

I wanted Stephen home, safe and secure. So I went searching on my bicycle—I was aware of the possible harmful effects of volcanic ash on car engines. When I returned, his bicycle was in the driveway. As usual, he hadn't put it where it belonged.

We watched the television coverage and set out cookie sheets to catch the descending ash so we could save some. For several days it was us against the forces of nature. We felt closer to one another than we usually did when skies were clear and bright. The problems *outside* seemed so much greater than the minor irritations inside the house that we got along marvelously. I wish I could handle an interruption that effectively every week!

However, most interruptions don't come on such a grand scale. Most are small and pesky, like mosquitoes. They require a patient, creative approach. But if I am unable to accept interruptions gracefully and sometimes even gloriously, I ought never to have become a parent. It may be, in fact, that my effectiveness as a father is measured by what I make of the interruptions.

Each day, my plans call for me to enjoy whatever the Lord and His six blessings have up their sleeves. Who knows, between the interruptions I may even get some work done.

"I will bless the Lord at all times: his praise shall continually be in my mouth" (Ps. 34:1).

Ten

HOTDOGS BY CANDLELIGHT

It had been a trying week for Mom. She had coordinated Girl
Scout cookie sales, recruited volunteers to staff the church nursery, served as room mother for a school party, as well as the normal stuff one must do as a parent of six healthy children: twenty-
five loads of laundry with all the socks turned inside out; seven
sets of sheets to wrestle off the beds; and dozens of trips by
Mom's 24-Hour Taxi Service. She was going to be late arriving
home that evening, so Dad and the kids decided to surprise her
by preparing an elegant dinner.

A major problem surfaced immediately: there was nothing re-
motely resembling elegant on the shelves or freezer. All we could
locate were two packages of hotdogs. What could we do?

So we made the best of it! Sara peeled carrots and cut them
into jagged sticks. Youngest son David set the table, folding napkins into unique shapes. Amy searched the cupboards and found
a big can of pork and beans and a bag of barbecue-flavored
chips. Stephen and Michael wrapped the hotdogs in biscuit mix
to create "pigs in a blanket." Dad cleaned up the sticky messes,
then rummaged with John in Mom's room for decorations. The
leftover candles found formed a rainbow of color on the dining
room table.

"Hurry! Mom's coming!" someone yelled. "I just heard the car in the driveway." We finished lighting the candles, turned off all the lights, and waited anxiously. It seemed as if hours passed before the doorknob turned and she came inside.

"Surprise, Mom!" we all shouted.

Hotdogs by candlelight were very special that night. Even Amy (who dislikes hotdogs with a passion) ate and enjoyed it. I chose not to notice that the neck of the catsup bottle was gooey from repeated spills; that somebody near me crunched carrot sticks with vigor; and that Amy sneaked the end of her hotdog into the waiting mouth of Max, our white and brown terrier. Dessert consisted of stale, crumbled vanilla wafers and scrapings from several nearly empty ice-cream cartons. Everybody had enough to eat.

I actually heard them say, "That was the best meal we've had in a long time."

It certainly wasn't because of the food. It must have been the mood. We had made the most of the little we had at the end of the month. And we had done it with style. I'm reminded of Solomon's proverb which says (freely translated), "Better to eat hotdogs by candlelight with people you love, than sirloin steak, baked potatoes, and sour cream amidst bickering and fighting" (Prov. 15:17).

Simple things seem to touch this father most deeply. Holding the soft hand of a child brings me a brighter glow within than tightly clasping a check made out in my name, no matter how many zeros follow the first number. Going to a movie extravaganza, though exciting, cannot compare to the novel productions our children periodically plan. I can tell they're up to something. They spend the whole day covertly preparing costumes, applying makeup, writing invitations, and rehearsing. At the appointed time, Mom and I (and any other persons who show the slightest interest—even some who don't) are escorted to the couch. Music blares from the tape deck. Though not all of their plays are comedies, I always seem to want to laugh. Quite often, the kids schedule their productions when I have truckloads of work to do. I have to concentrate on relaxing during such glorious interruptions. Before long, I've forgotten my pressing duties, and these "stars" have pranced and giggled their way into my heart.

I have frequently experienced disappointment on our family's major excursions. Perhaps it's the pressure of trying to get everything ready. Perhaps it's the noise which escalates too far in advance of departure time, causing my nerves to be jangled beyond repair. Maybe I have built up my expectations unreasonably high. It could be just plain old tired-outness. All I know is that the simple, spontaneous, inexpensive events enter most profoundly into my soul. Here are some of the best:

Having my kindergartner snuggle beside me, reading his first book. He hesitates often but makes it through, beaming with pride. "See, Dad? I told you I could read."

Receiving an extra long, extra hard bedtime hug when I bend over to kiss her good-night, even if she is stalling for time.

Everybody talking at once during dinner, each one recounting the day's happenings. Amazingly, I catch almost every detail.

Giving the dogs a bath in the backyard. We all get soaked from their shaking, but laughter resounds as one child hangs on, another scrubs, and a third dries the wet fur with an old towel.

Making ice cream. When one short arm grows weary, another is ready to turn the crank. As I crush ice cubes with a hammer and sprinkle rock salt, I try to explain how it works—a neat trick, since I only vaguely understand. I know how to eat it, though. The wooden beater is a prime treat. We issue spoons and everybody scrapes as fast as possible.

In spite of such simple delights, I suppose we'll continue to plan big events. For eldest son John's sixteenth birthday, we're going to travel across the Cascade Mountains to Seattle to see a professional basketball game. I'll likely be tense much of the time as I worry, *Will we find a parking place? Can we really afford this? Are they out too late on a school night? What if I can't find where I parked the car? And . . .*

It is certain to be a thrilling adventure. But it will never take the place of holding hands, hugging at bedtime, squeezes, bathing dogs, cranking ice cream, watching the kids' dramatic productions, or eating hotdogs by candlelight.

"... the living God ... giveth us richly all things to enjoy" (1 Tim. 6:17).

Eleven

THE TUG OF WAR BETWEEN HOME AND JOB

I feel the pull both ways. I go to work remembering all the things I need to do at home; I come home unable to forget the un-finished tasks at the office. It's quite a tug of war. Sometimes I feel strong and can hold myself together. I'm usually effective in both places, accomplishing the major goals concurrently. Then along comes a moment of weariness and I yield to whichever side pulls harder. Usually that's my work outside the home. I wish it weren't so, but I'm being paid to produce. There are persons to whom I am immediately accountable. And there are others waiting in the wings to take my place.

Meanwhile back at home, they'll still love me if I have to miss an important event in their lives. They'll, of course, be disappoint-ed. But they understand Dad has his work to do. After all, they and I need to eat, make house payments and have clothes to wear. So, sometimes, I put in overtime at the job and undertime with the family.

Children don't have much clout. They can't demand forty hours a week from me. They don't have the power to replace or fire me. They can tune me out, stop respecting me, and search for fatherly affection elsewhere. But they can't vote me out of office.

It's up to me to figure out a way to win at this tug of war. It's either that or I'd better let go of the rope and quit playing the silly game. Under the prevailing rules, when one side is victorious, the other side loses. But I want everyone to win. I don't want either side to be dragged through the mud. So how do I go about accomplishing this? How do I ensure that I'm in peak form when at home? I have three secrets.

1. Concentration

When I'm home I'm really home, not only with my body but with my mind and affections as well. I try to listen with undivided attention to what the kids say. I seek to be responsive to their needs.

On my typing desk is a favorite gift: a plastic figurine of Snoopy. On its stand is inscribed, "World's Greatest." It fails to say world's greatest *what,* so I am free to use my imagination—I am not a world-class athlete, a great inventor, scientist or wage earner. Some days, however, I feel like I am one of the world's best fathers. I'm involved intimately in their lives, caring and encouraging; wiping tears from rosy cheeks; doling out "give me five" hand slaps; carrying them to bed piggy back; delivering eloquent if ineffective lectures on the joys of homework.

My Snoopy is flying his imaginary Sopwith Camel, with teeth clenched, and tail and ascot streaming behind. He's wearing a helmet and goggles because he's on the move and flying high. Sure, everybody knows he's actually earthbound, going nowhere. But Snoopy doesn't care what the rest of the world thinks or sees. He's heading into an adventure, a dogfight to end all dogfights, and he's up to his floppy little ears in excitement.

That's what I want: to be so involved with and excited about my family that I don't hear the alluring call of the big world outside. I want to be having such a great time as a father that nothing could entice me away.

I took daughter Sara shopping for a birthday gift one evening. I would have preferred sitting in my overstuffed chair, shoes off, newspaper spread across my lap, eyes at half mast. Instead, I made use of this necessary errand to enjoy some time with her.

She rummaged through toys, books, records, jewelry, hair clips and other possibilities. I stood back and followed her seven-year-old body and mind as she wandered the aisles. She eventually made a final decision. Then it was over to the greeting cards. Sara is attracted to adult cards with crinkly parchment paper, pink roses and sunsets behind purple mountains. The pictures are all right but I cannot stand the trite messages. This time I convinced her to buy a card with three cute kittens. We accomplished our purpose and both of us felt good. I was able to dump my awareness of other commitments and just be with her. We concentrated on each other and were rewarded by a warm and special experience.

2. Accomplishment

Sometimes my soul is in imminent danger of unraveling, and I can't find a knot or even a tangle to hold it together. For such moments, I have discovered the secret of accomplishment. I look for a small, manageable job which I can finish in a short length of time. So I line up shoes in my closet, or wipe toothpaste spatters off the bathroom mirror, or pick up hangers from the closet floor, or put new shoestrings in somebody's sneakers, or water a few house plants. The roof may be caving in, the car falling apart, my tax return overdue, and our yard a national disaster area. But I feel super. I have just done something useful. I feel good about myself again.

I'm not implying that a parent ought to look for ways to avoid important jobs such as cleaning the oven or defrosting the freezer. It's simply my way of coping while waiting for the proper moment in which to tackle the biggies. Thus, I'm able to be reasonably "together" as a father.

3. Forgetting

I forget people's names with ease; I even forget my own children's names when I'm upset. I also forget appointments, phone numbers, and where I parked the car at the shopping center. I often forget to buy some of the groceries on the list Ellen so carefully compiled.

But I'm referring here to something other than routine lapses in memory. I'm talking about *emotional* forgetting. When one (or more) of our children becomes angry at me, I need to accept the validity of his feelings; and I don't have to carry around my response of anger, hurt, or guilt the rest of the day. I can *choose* not to remember. I do not just forget by the mere passage of time or by immersing myself in busyness. I decide not to store up bitterness, not to hang onto disappointment, not to clutch sadness to my heart. In the course of any given day, enough hurtful things are said that if I were to store them within, I would probably never smile again. So I choose to forget. I don't always pull it off. But when I do, it sets me free to communicate openly, to love without reservation.

In the rapid movement of family life today, I don't have the luxury of nursing my negative feelings. That's why I'm working to perfect the art of quickly forgetting.

I don't have any magic answers. I do know it doesn't feel good to be caught in a tug of war between my family and my job. If either wants to make a wish, let him find a turkey bone on which to pull, but I'm off to practice what I preach. Ah, that it were so easy!

I shall attempt to concentrate on their needs, be involved in their projects, and listen to what they have to say. I shall search for a neat little task to do so I can gain a sense of accomplishment. I shall forget the slights and hurts.

"I will walk within my house with a perfect heart" (Ps. 101:2b).

Twelve

I MUMBLE AT LITTLE LEAGUE GAMES

Three of our four boys have played Little League baseball. Number four will be eligible this year. Amy, Sara and Michael play soccer. Eldest son, John, bowls every Saturday morning. Stephen wrestles and plays football. All of them have made an attempt in track. None is a fantastic athlete, but all six are strong and healthy. As interested parents, Ellen and I gallantly try to attend every one of their athletic events. Sometimes three kids are playing soccer on three different fields on three different sides of town. We wave to each other on the road as we switch games at halftimes, trying to see part of each child's match.

I cannot begin to estimate how many hours I've spent watching our kids participate in sporting events. But I can say I've enjoyed nearly every minute. I'm a loyal fan, sitting in the bleachers or standing by the sidelines, rooting for my kids—even in the worst of weather.

I'm not a yeller at games. I get very emotionally charged, but I don't jump up and down and scream. I just sit and mumble, too softly to bother anyone except my wife. Thus, I don't embarrass my budding athlete by making a fool of myself. I just bring Ellen to a state of nervous exhaustion as I mutter my suggestions and complaints. I am an accomplished mumbler. "He called that a strike? It was a foot too high."

"If I were the coach" is a fun game. It's safe to play, and I create my own results. My mumbled coaching decisions from the stands are 100 percent accurate.

Before you self-righteously condemn my behavior, let me offer an explanation. You'd mumble, too, if someone kept breaking your concentration to ask questions. I sometimes feel as though I'm conducting a clinic on sports terminology and theory.

"Why is the man in the striped shirt waving his arms like a windmill?" Ellen asks.

"Because the right guard, who happens to be our son, moved out of his three-point stance before the ball was snapped."

"Well, they shouldn't expect him to stay in that uncomfortable position so long."

"He has to remain there until the center hikes the ball."

"It doesn't seem fair. Those boys on the other team are standing up and moving around all they want."

"They're on defense, dear. They have to obey the same rule when they have the ball."

"So why is number 22 running? The ball is still on the ground."

"He's in motion. One player in the backfield may start running before the ball is snapped, as long as he runs parallel with the line of scrimmage."

"But the ball isn't on a line. It's halfway between."

"The line of scrimmage is an imaginary line drawn across the front tip of the football." My voice trails off into my muttering routine.

I mumble when things go badly for our team, such as the time Stephen was pitching and the score was 23-2 in favor of the *other* guys—in the second inning. I think the game was called off out of compassion. Then in the very next outing, he pitched a gem of a game, striking out sixteen batters in six innings. I used my loud and proud mumble, informing people that was *my* son on the mound—humbly, of course.

I mumble because I care. At a football game last fall, our son was obviously the best player on the field. He did it all: recovered a fumble, intercepted a pass, blocked crisply, and tackled with authority. Other parents didn't seem to understand and praised the accomplishments of their sons. Couldn't they see that *my* son was clearly best, the star? I had no choice but to start mumbling about how certain players seldom get the recognition they deserve.

I have also perfected the use of the mumble during games around the house. Wrestling with my kids is an activity where it comes in handy. "Hey, Dad, wanna wrestle?" Three boys eagerly await my reply, their eyes sparkling and muscles flexing.

"Well, maybe for a short while." The words are hardly out of my mouth before they're pulling me outside. In the good old days, I was able to pick them up and twirl them around. No more. One grabs my legs, another jumps on my back, the third tugs on my arm. Down I go, careful not to crush someone. I have greater strength but they have stamina; that is, they don't know when to quit. When I sense my body growing weary, I commence mumbling. "Aren't you kids ready to give up?" What a silly question.

Waiting is the activity that brings out the most mumbling. Being a parent isn't all glamour and excitement. It involves a lot of standing around or sitting in the car. "How much longer is soccer practice going to last?" I mutter to myself. "I have other things I need to do." So I wait while they finish their piano or ice-skating lessons, band rehearsals and sessions with the orthodontist.

I finally decided I ought to put my waiting to better purpose than merely mumbling and grumbling. I call it creative waiting. If I can't doze for a few moments to refresh myself, I take my pad and pencil and do a little writing. I sometimes meditate, studying the green hills or unique cloud formations. I pray for other parents who wait and whose faces grow more tense by the minute. Or I enjoy a brief daydream. There is a father in the Scriptures who waited longer than I ever have, and whose hope was rewarded when the son returned (Luke 15:11-32). So I might as well wait in style since I have little control over the situations. Eventually they'll show up, if for no other reason than that of the prodigal son—hunger pangs.

"I'm here, Dad," my daughter announces. "Let's go home."

"Okay, but you'll have to wait. I'm not quite finished day-dreaming."

"Let the words of my mouth, and the meditation of my heart, be acceptable in thy sight, O Lord, my strength, and my redeemer" (Ps. 19:14).

Thirteen

GRAVESIDE SERVICES WILL BE UNDER THE PEACH TREE

We buried Michael's hamster under the peach tree by a corner of the house. David and Sara had decorated a shoe box with
crayon designs and construction paper. We carefully placed Ike's
furry corpse amidst several sheets of tissue. I tied down the lid
with string. Amy picked a bouquet of pink and white peonies. The
tragedy occurred in May, so the peach tree was bringing comfort
by sharing its delicate blossoms. Music was provided by birds
singing melodies of joy from a cherry tree just across the fence.
Though past their prime, two lilac bushes offered their fragrance.

We held a brief but meaningful ceremony as our family stood
in our freshly spaded garden. Here and there green shoots in neat
rows peeked from beneath the soil, showing promise of leafy lettuce or crisp red radishes. Michael's face contorted with grief. But
we did not think and talk only of death, for everywhere around us
was the life and beauty of spring. I commended Ike to wherever
hamster souls go. We dug a hole and gently laid the shoe box in
it. Michael insisted he be the one to shovel dirt and fill the grave.
He marked the mound by placing on it a favorite white rock from
his prized collection. A cardboard sign announced "Ike" in sec-
ond-grade printing. We stuck the peonies in the ground and then
reminisced.

About a year and a half before, John and Michael had desperately wanted something living and cute. John had his heart set on

a boa constrictor. Ellen declared, "You'd better call the snake 'Mom,' because if it comes to live here, you'll never see me again."

The pet store assistant helped us select two hamsters which he guaranteed were male. John christened his Peppy. Mike chose the name Ike. Several weeks later I went out of town for a church convention. When I returned, the kids first asked what I had brought for them. (When I'm away for any extended length of time, I try to bring home small gifts or treats to reward their patience and for having helped Mom.) I distributed the gifts and sat down to listen to all the things I had missed in their busy young lives. They can quickly forget what nine-times-eight equals, yet recall every minute detail of their last three soccer games. Michael could hardly wait to show me Ike.

"You've got to see how much my hamster has grown," he said proudly. "He's twice as big as John's. I must be doing a super job!" We went to the cage for a look. My suspicions were aroused when I noticed the part of Ike that was growing, so I picked up the furry critter for a closer examination.

"Mike, I think you ought to know something. Ike is a *she,* a female. She's going to have babies and probably very soon." We rushed out to buy another cage to set her up in housekeeping. Within twenty-four hours the blessed event occurred. She delivered eight tiny, hairless creatures with tightly shut eyes, who squirmed all over her and each other. At that point the story took a sad turn—Ike ate her babies. I shall spare you the sordid details. Suffice it to say we will never again consent to being hamster midwives. Actually, we didn't consent the first time.

Ike lived to a ripe old age, as hamster chronology goes. The children handled the loss quite well, honestly expressing their feelings. They accepted her death as a normal part of the cycle of life.

I'm amazed at how children can cope with death. The day Grandma Emert died, I was in my office when word reached me. I hurried home. There in the living room were Ellen and seven-year-old Sara. They were on the couch, with Sara sitting on her mom's lap, arms wrapped around her mother's neck. Thank goodness I had the wisdom not to interrupt. It was a precious moment.

One of them would divulge a memory about Grandma and

they would either laugh or cry. Then another would add a thought. Sometimes laughter and crying seemed intertwined. They recalled that Grandma enjoyed crossword puzzles, paperback romances and yellow roses; that she always brought angel food cake for Christmas dinner. Sara mentioned the crisp dollar bills tucked in her birthday cards and visits to Grandma's apartment after school. "Tell us what it was like when you were a little girl—like the time you rode in a covered wagon from Idaho." The grandchildren learned a great deal from her. They would lie on the carpet listening to her tales or studying the globe she kept by her rocking chair. Her candy jar always had something sweet inside. It made a telltale clink when we lifted the glass lid.

The funeral service was wonderful and helpful. But I think Sara, snuggled upon Ellen's lap, brought more comfort than all the words of sympathy, floral arrangements and gracious cards put together. As the prophet Isaiah so aptly observes, ". . . a little child shall lead them" (Isa. 11:6d, RSV).

No family is immune from disappointments and sorrows. We still feel twinges of pain when thinking of how our faithful dog, Eve, died. She had been a family member for all of her fifteen years. In fact, she was our first "child." Having grown feeble, she chose a dark summer night to wander away and not return.

Then there was that slippery tropical fish that apparently gave one mighty leap right out of the tank. We found its dried remains several days later. There was also the brightly plumed parakeet whose perch was too close to an outside door during school spring vacation. The constant coming and going of kids caused a draft which brought on a case of pneumonia.

The hurt of such loss is real because the love is real. And even if I could protect them from the pain, I shouldn't try. We need to experience the grief together so that together God might heal us. "Blessed are those who mourn," said Jesus, "for they shall be comforted" (Matt. 5:4, RSV).

"To every thing there is a season, and a time to every purpose under the heaven: a time to be born, and a time to die. . ." (Eccles. 3:1-2).

Fourteen

BUMPS, GROANS AND SOUNDS IN THE NIGHT

God could have created humans able to live without sleep. It would have meant continuous activity, twenty-four hours a day. However, in His mercy God took pity on parents. After some of the days I endure as their dad, I need to tiptoe into their various rooms to observe them at sleep.

The daylight hours may have been catastrophic:
> dirty socks and chicken pox; extra noise and broken toys; an unexpected bill and "Why can't they sit still?"

I may have missed my lunch and heard something in the car go crunch;
> found smudges on the kitchen wall and a window shattered by a ball.

But if I can sneak beside their beds and gaze for a moment, my faith is restored, hope springs again within my heart. *"My, aren't they precious? Such sweet children, so peaceful and beautiful."*

Wait just a minute! Aren't these the same kids who an hour ago were plundering the house? Terrorizing the neighborhood? Spilling dinner on the dining room rug? Feeding the dog Brussels sprouts? Getting mud stuck in the tread of their tennis shoes? (Have you tried to clean mud from the bottom of tennis shoes? More than once I've seriously considered throwing them away and buying a new pair.) Yep, same kids. It's amazing how quickly I forget their misdeeds once they're safely tucked under the covers.

Thank the Lord that kids need more sleep than parents. I cherish those few hours at night after all the little bodies are at rest. We two bigger bodies then carry on adult conversations amidst peace and quiet. I watch whatever I want on television. I doze without fear of somebody jumping on my unsuspecting tummy. I make thick sandwich creations and no one turns up his nose and says "Yuk!" I boldly enter the kitchen to get a cookie or a bowl of ice cream. Earlier in the day such endeavors require stealth and cunning; at night there's no need to be anything but my lazy self. After bedtime, no child's eyes are watching my every move, and no impressionable young mind is adopting my behavior as a pattern.

There's one small problem. They seldom remain peaceful for the duration of the night. They emit strange noises: teeth grind, noses whistle, and other parts of the anatomy provide bumps, groans, thuds and moans. Quite an orchestra! There are other sounds, such as the radio that teenage Steve left on. Number three on the hit parade may lull him to dreamland—it would drive me to the funny farm. When we had hamsters, there was the constant squeaking of the exercise wheel—I vainly tried every lubricant known to science. Those rodents are smarter than their beady eyes indicate. What a great system: sleep all day while the kids are around, then get up when all is peaceful.

Parents learn to sleep with certain parts of their bodies while other parts stay alert. "Okay, right ear. It's your turn to be on duty tonight." We become accustomed to routine sounds, so it takes an out-of-the-ordinary noise to rouse you. One dark winter morning, when Amy was three years old, we heard a scream. Ellen and I jumped from bed, eyes still shut but feet moving. There was Amy standing on the kitchen counter, below the cupboard where the cookie jar was located. She couldn't climb down. Panic at 3 a.m.

I'm so good at selective listening that I hardly stir when footsteps patter down the hall to the bathroom. But let the footsteps be toward the kitchen, and I take notice. After all, Dad has certain inalienable rights, one being an exclusive on nocturnal refrigerator raids. After school, it's open season on refrigerators; let 'em make off with what they can. When the sun goes down, however, it's all mine.

The following fact defies logic. When we've managed to farm them all out on the same night, Dad and Mom get a great night's sleep, right? Wrong! We toss and turn, listening for sounds that aren't there. It's too quiet. I should make a tape recording some noisy night so I can replay it when they're gone. This might become a profitable business venture. Surely other lonely parents would buy a tape. It would be cheaper and healthier than taking sleeping pills.

Right now I'm having a difficult period of adjustment. We have teens in the family who have a primordial urge to stay up late. "But, Dad, that's when the really good shows are on. The earlier ones are kid stuff." Perhaps, but I still need my alone time, staring blankly at a test pattern in the wee hours. No matter how great the sacrifice, I'm going to get my quota of peace and quiet.

I figure it this way. On his travels, Gulliver made only one mistake. He (the big person) went to sleep before they (the little ones) did. And they tied him up. I don't intend to err in that manner. No matter how tired I become, I'll stay awake long enough to select my very own television show and to raid the refrigerator at least once.

If you ever want to pick me out of a crowd, look for a pudgy dad who's rubbing his bleary eyes.

"Yet the Lord will command his lovingkindness in the daytime, and in the night his song shall be with me, and my prayer unto the God of my life" (Ps. 42:8).

Fifteen

"UP YOUR NOSE WITH A RUBBER HOSE" AND OTHER SWEET NOTHINGS

Where in the world do they learn these maledictions?
"Last one's a rotten egg!"
"Your mother wears combat boots!"
"Up your nose with a rubber hose!"
We didn't teach our children such sweet nothings, I assure you. Mom and I have labored long to instill responses such as, "Please," "Thank you," and "May I be excused." And our kids do employ good verbal manners, although I suspect it's when they know we're within hearing range. But "Stick it in your ear" and "Hang it on your beak" seem to spring spontaneously from their chromosomes.

Not only do they know the proper improper words; they intuitively know how to speak them. Nasal tones, squinty eyes, and contorted lip accompany their delivery. Ask them to read great poetry and they stumble through with little feeling, and with hardly any sense of rhyme or rhythm. But their timing is precise, their diction immaculate, their pitch perfect as they yell, "Nee-nur-nee-nur-nee-nurr! In your eye with a chocolate cream pie!"

I'll wager not one of our children has ever seen a rotten egg. That's no impediment, however, to the free usage of a phrase with those words. It's a very flexible invective. Should one happen to be at the back of the pack, he simply hollers, "First one's a rotten egg!" Obviously, the best place to be is in the middle, but the child with his or her mouth open has the advantage. He must never shout until victory is assured. Just before he steps through the door, he turns, sneers, and says, "Last one in the house is a rotten egg!" Then as the others enter, he condescendingly adds, "Too bad, you lost." And small children with high-pitched voices can effectively compete with larger, stronger kids.

It's quite a challenge to help form their developing vocabularies. How come slang words (or worse) make indelible impressions in their memory banks, while kind, pleasant terms seem to pass through without a trace? For a while I advocated washing the mouth with soap. I no longer do, realizing that the problem is not in the mouth but in the mind and heart of the child. Jesus made it clear that ". . . the mouth speaks what the heart is full of. A good person brings good things out of his treasure of good things" (Matt. 12:34b-35a, TEV).

Innocent Sara sweetly inquired at the dinner table, "Mommy, what does ———— mean?" The other five children, who had all been talking with food in their mouths, fell silent. Not even a gulp or a swallow was heard. All eyes were focused on Mother, who was nearly choking on her macaroni and cheese. She glanced desperately in my direction, her face white with panic. I managed to suppress a laugh. I could tell she was not finding the moment very amusing.

"Uh-h-h, Sara dear, why don't you ask your father after dinner is over? I'm sure he can give you a better answer than I."

She managed that hand-off as smoothly as any professional quarterback ever did. She looked relieved. Chewing and talking resumed. Then the thought occurred to me, *Why does she think I can deal with such matters better than she? Does she believe I'm able to discuss topics like this with less embarrassment? At least if I eat slowly, I'll have some time in which to formulate my response. And maybe Sara will forget all about it, particularly if we have something special for dessert.*

"Mom, John called me a nerd."

"John, did you call your sister a name?"

"Who, me? Naw, I just said she was a nerd."

"Would you please explain what a nerd is?"

"How should I know? But everybody's using it."

"Well, that doesn't mean you have to. Try to be more thought-ful."

Such conversations are frequent in a houseful of kids. The dictionary is of no help. As soon as adults define the meanings of young people's vocabulary, the whippersnappers create new ones. Of course, certain words will never fall into the generation gap. "Dirty rat," "dummy," "you stink," and "liar, liar, pants on fire" are in this category. Kids may forget all the rules of grammar, but they remember how to cast insults. They may not learn the correct usage of semicolons, yet they can quickly string adjectives together, such as in, "You rotten, no-good, lousy ..."

I have difficulty accepting their crude use of English; I also have trouble coping with some of their positive expressions. When I learned to read, I delighted in sentences like, "See Dick run. See Spot run. See Dick, Jane, and Spot run." I enjoyed the stories, though I couldn't figure out why Dick, Jane, and Spot were never out of breath from all the running they did. Well, times have changed. Kids don't talk like kids anymore. They use polysyllabic words and often speak with technological jargon.

I overheard David (when he was about four) say to his mom, "You are unable to spank me because I'm totally surrounded by an impregnable force field." What he didn't know, however, is that mothers have a force field of their very own. He got spanked, although Mom seemed to have difficulty trying to spank and keep from laughing at the same time. David's talk is sprinkled with words such as "hyperspace," "digital read-out," and "instantaneous disintegration." It's scary. A mop-haired kid looks me in the belt buckle and solemnly informs me that lasers travel in an absolutely straight line. He doesn't intend to make me feel dumb, but I do. And what's worse, I think I know the reason why: I am.

Fortunately, parental success is not based solely on intelligence, on keeping current with the latest youth slang, nor on ability to understand *Star Wars* vintage lingo. I bring home a paycheck, know how to housebreak a dog, and can do a Windsor knot on a tie. I don't care whether kids wear ties or not; I find a measure of solace in being able to yell, "Last one to tie his necktie is a rotten egg."

"A word fitly spoken is like apples of gold in pictures of silver" (Prov. 25:11).

Sixteen

THE TROUBLE WITH THE WORLD IS INSIDE-OUT SOCKS

I was trying to be a helpful husband. Ellen had over-volunteered her time at school, church and Bluebirds (If a community figures out they have a real, live volunteer in their midst, they declare open season on her), so I bounded down the steps to the laundry room, three at a time. I felt like such a wonderful person as I tackled the mountain of dirty clothes heaped in the basket and flooding onto the floor.

Perhaps I should explain that my degree is in theology and not in clothes-sorting. I did know, however, that darks should be washed separately from whites. I had read the instructions on the box to determine how much detergent to use. And it wasn't my first encounter with the machine, so I knew how to operate the dials.

Everything went well at the beginning. At the top of the pile were larger articles such as pants, shirts, dresses and jeans. I remembered to check pockets, and found it to be an exciting venture. Strange things lurk in pockets of a little boy's denims. I pulled out a rusty nail and several flattened bottle caps, a broken comb, crumpled homework assignments, a piece of previously chewed gum, and cookie crumbs galore. Fascinating! Luckily, there were no living creatures tucked away, although a leftover-sandwich crust was starting to grow mold.

I proceeded to the lower levels of the clothes heap. Incredible. There was a pretzelized jumble of socks, twisted into all kinds of colorful lumps. An unpleasant odor drifted upward. I dug in, my enthusiasm rapidly waning, as I breathed through my mouth to avoid smelling the toxic air.

When I had finished the task, I was exhausted. There must have been a thousand socks in that basket, and not one was right-side out. I had to reach my hand inside each one, grab the toe and pull. I nearly lost my appetite. Fortunately (or unfortunately, when I look at my profile in the mirror), it takes more than that to squelch my appetite.

My back wearied from bending over at this labor of love. If it had been somebody else's kids who had worn those socks, I would have handled the mess by remote control. I have a new appreciation for towels. There is no way a child can turn a towel inside out.

A great truth slowly dawned as I reached inside a sock that must have been worn all week—for Phy. Ed., through mud puddles, and as a dust mop. *The problem with the world is that everybody turns his dirty socks inside out.* It was a beautiful symbol (well, not beautiful, but accurate). A difficulty in our society is persons who are not thoughtful of others. "What's wrong with dumping my small bit of litter beside the road? Nobody will ever notice." Sure, one pair of inside-out socks doesn't seem like much. But multiply that by several million and you've got a national crisis.

I'm convinced that what's wrong today is not only what headlines and TV announcers boldly proclaim. It's not only tension in the Middle East, nuclear proliferation, high unemployment, or a belt-tightening recession. It's inside-out socks, as simple as that. It's the little things which put us in a dither, those minor irritations which cause indigestion and ulcers.

The problem with the world is a doorknob with gooey handprints; a windshield wiper that clatters; service station attendants that splash gas on the fender; a person who cuts in at a fast-food restaurant; and a guy who idles his car five seconds after the light turns green.

The problem with the world is a fellow worker's Monday morning grouchiness; the evening paper thrown into the bushes; a flat tire when I'm already late for an appointment.

The problem with the world is toothpaste on the bathroom mirror; white dog hairs on a navy blue blazer; a frayed shoelace that won't fit through the eye no matter how much I lick and twist it; an empty toilet paper roll.

I have several options as a father and as a member of the human race. I can shake my fist at God for having created feet which get cold and therefore need socks. I can move my family into the backwoods where we can go barefoot. I can try to isolate myself from others and insulate my feelings. Or I can accept my lot in life. I can draw a deep breath (preferably far from the clothes hamper) and pray for guidance. I can recognize that fatherhood necessarily means encounters with life's little irritations.

Like it or not, I shall sometimes experience my children in their unexpurgated versions. My love is relatively untested by the sweet, clean child with curly locks and frilly dress, or with ironed shirt and neatly combed hair. But if I wish to discover how strong my love really is, bring me a kid with raspberry Jell-O dried in his hair, with fingernails that could grow carrots in the dirt underneath them, or with licorice ice cream smeared from ear to ear. Unconditional love is hugging that child—hard.

Unconditional love is reaching inside dirty socks to put them right side out again.

Perhaps if everybody would just turn his own socks right side out, there might be harmony and peace on earth. It might not instantly resolve tensions between the United States and Russia, but at least it would relax one dad I know. And since it's been the fathers and sons who have fought in all the wars, maybe I've stumbled upon a key to making this the best of all possible worlds.

If the Hebrews in the first century had worn socks with their sandals, perhaps the Master would have added another Beatitude: "Blessed are those who turn their dirty socks right side out. . . ."

"Thou shalt love thy neighbour as thyself" (Matt. 19:19b).

Seventeen

CATCH THE SPILLED MILK BEFORE IT REACHES THE CRACK!

His short arms are trying to reach halfway across the table. "I want some jelly," he says as he keeps stretching. In a prone position, it's almost inevitable that his shirt will sag into the potatoes and gravy. Then his glass of milk tips over. Why is it glasses are never knocked over when they're empty, only when they're full?

Spilled milk instantly mobilizes our family. Everyone throws his napkin in the direction the spill is flowing. Dad hustles into the kitchen to grab some paper towels while Mom builds a dike by the crack in the table (How did mankind survive before paper towels?). Our dining room table has two expansion leaves, and therefore three cracks. Liquid spilled on any part of the table automatically heads toward the nearest crevice.

The guilty party explains why it wasn't his fault. "If Mike had passed the jelly when I first asked, I wouldn't have reached so far. And anyway, who put my glass there? Somebody moved it." In unison, the family responds, "Not me!"

Dad grumbles about how expensive milk is as he crawls under the table to check for drips. He makes the final test by rubbing the carpet beneath the crack. It's dry this time. Amy pours more milk for little brother. Tears are wiped by one of the napkins Sara brings from the kitchen drawer. Dinner resumes. The kids are quieter than usual for a short while.

I have decided it's best to expect the unexpected in this family. If I figure things will be normal and calm, with milk glasses remaining upright, I am doomed to disappointment. I panic rather than cope. Instead of scolding the child while the milk wends its inexorable way toward the crack, it's far better to grab the towels and start mopping. There's always time later to deliver the required fatherly lecture. My kids could probably repeat those pep talks verbatim. The following is a reasonable facsimile of a speech on the evils of spilling milk: "I'm not blaming you, son, but milk is not cheap these days, and neither are paper towels and napkins. Furthermore, sour milk on the carpet is bad news. So please be more careful from now on. If you had asked rather than reached for the jelly, this whole mess would have been avoided." Then turning to the entire assembly, I wail, "How many times do accidents have to happen before anybody learns?" I know, it's not a brilliant question. But I can't seem to keep from asking it.

My mother, bless her heart, visited us later that day, and informed the world that when "your daddy was a little boy, he spilled more milk than all six of you combined." Grandparents are neat people. If only they wouldn't tell so much about us parents.

Thousands of household accidents occur each year. I'm amazed there aren't more. Disasters far greater than a little puddle of milk are lurking in the shadows, awaiting an unsuspecting parent. One glance at our garage should convince even the skeptical. Trikes, bikes, wagon tongues, roller skates, rake handles, boxes, and assorted junk create a formidable obstacle course. I travel through at my own risk, especially after dark. Bicycle pedals are particularly vicious.

Inside the house lurk more hazards. Fallen coat hangers, bent into strange shapes, grapple ankles that enter the closet. Shoes and boots strewn in the hallway try to entangle feet. The worst danger? I've never read an article warning about those lethal toys called jacks. Anybody who has ever stepped on one with bare feet knows the full meaning of pain. Soldiers should be issued a pouch of jacks. They could spread a few on the enemy's path and wait for cries of "Yeow!" and "I-yi-yi!"

Another potential risk is the common telephone cord. It's totally safe when the receiver is cradled on the phone and the cord is tucked neatly beside it. However, it is seldom in this position around our house. Usually a teenager has the receiver in his or her sweaty hand and is cloistered out of sight, around the corner in the living room, on the stairs, or on the floor. The victim (Dad) approaches. The cord strikes, tripping and entrapping my body like some skinny boa constrictor.

Even the most utilitarian of objects can turn on me. Sara came down to breakfast the other morning in her typically deliberate manner. "You know how I'm always the last one to go to the bathroom?" I nodded agreement. "Well, um-m-m, I was the last one again today, and, uh—" she paused to look at the ceiling, "I think there's a problem."

"Oh? What kind of problem?" She had my undivided attention.

"I think it's running over."

"It's what? Why didn't you tell me?" I set my coffee cup down and dashed to the bathroom. A shy voice trailed after me.

"Dad, I just did."

Thankfully, it hadn't run over.

We parents must come to these moments of tension with a positive attitude and a liberal dose of good humor. We can complain because our children's shoes wear out too fast; or we can rejoice that our kids are healthy, growing and on the move. We can grump about their noise and interruptions; or we can give thanks for their energy and lung power.

Attitude is a product of inner life. My moods are not dependent on the kids' behavior. Of course, I experience emotional fluctuations, relative to their sorrows and joys. But I seek to love them with constancy, to provide for them faithfully, and to discipline them consistently.

I believe the joys of parenthood far outweigh the difficulties. Please note: I did not say *outnumber*, for that would be telling an untruth. Though the problems may come in truckloads and occur with great frequency, the joys of being a parent outweigh them by tons. I should know. I've checked the scales often.

The psalmist understood. He looked at his family one day and wrote, ". . . look at all those children! There they sit around the dinner table as vigorous and healthy as young olive trees. That is God's reward to those who reverence and trust him" (Ps. 128:3b-4, TLB). I thank God for rewarding me so richly, spilled milk included. After all, I could be somewhere in a lonely corner, eating my meals from a TV tray.

"Rejoice evermore. Pray without ceasing. In every thing give thanks: for this is the will of God in Christ Jesus concerning you" (1 Thess. 5:16-18).

Eighteen

THEY'RE ALL OURS

Fifty years ago a family of eight wasn't novel. By standards of farm families then, it would have been average size. Today it's different. I tell someone I have six children, and suddenly his eyebrows raise and he says with strangled tone, "You have *how many* children?"

We have confided in persons close to us that some of our children are adopted. But word seems to have traveled around our small community. That's to be expected. Therefore, it's relatively common to have someone inquire, "Which ones are adopted and which are yours?" At first I took offense, bristling inside but bridling my tongue. No more. I politely yet firmly say, "They're *all* ours. If you mean which are store bought and which are home grown, that's a separate matter." Most people take my correction in the spirit with which I offer it. The fact is, *they are all ours!* It might be more accurate, though, to say that we (Mom and Dad) are *theirs*; at least that's how it seems some days.

I'm not certain why folks are concerned about *how* we became a family. What counts is that we *are* a family, loving and communicating, engaged together in the joyful struggle of living. We are usually so busy being a family that we don't talk much about who came from where. We do sometimes rehearse birth dates, birthplaces, circumstances and interesting tidbits about their specific roots. They enjoy hearing such things, even if for the hundredth time. There are special memories connected to the arrival of each of our children, whether Ellen and I labored for her in the hospital or labored for him through an adoption agency and the courts. Work is work.

I seldom tell people which kids arrived by which method. "Figure it out," I say, "if you can." They usually cannot, which pleases me. It indicates we look and act like a family, and are not just a collection of warm bodies.

I want us as a family to deal honestly with our unique backgrounds, but finding proper labels is hard. I do not appreciate the term "natural children" to distinguish them from the adopted ones. It implies that adopted children, children by a previous marriage, or foster children are in some way unnatural. Not so! All children come naturally. The words we often use in discussing birth "status" are loaded with double standards, in a day when double standards are supposedly passé. For example, I prefer the phrase "*biological* parents" over "*real* parents." Exactly what have we been doing these sixteen years? Being "unreal," nonexistent parents? I'm aware that other persons brought three of our children into the world. I understand the agony of the decisions they made. And I know the joy of being entrusted with the responsibility to help these children mature. But please don't suggest that our love and labor as parents aren't real. I have the scars and the precious memories to prove they are.

It is sometimes intimated that one method of joining a family's ranks is superior to another. Different, yes. Superior, no. People must realize that Mom and Dad adopted one another. There is no biological tie (If there is, law requires it to be very distant). We *chose* each other. Our marriage is a mutual affair. Even more important, all of us in the family of God have been adopted. In his letter to the Romans, Paul writes, ". . . you have been adopted into the very family circle of God and you can say with a full heart, 'Father, my Father'" (Rom. 8:15, Phillips).

We don't try to hide the individuality of each child. Instead, we highlight the ways in which their beginnings, gifts, and unique qualities make each of them special. In day-to-day living, it makes not an iota of difference from where, when or how they came. We have invested the same amount of blood, sweat, tears and money in each. My emotional attachment knows nothing of origins. I chew my fingernails in equal measure for each child. I swell to the same size with pride at the accomplishments of all. These are my children. I love them, get angry at them, and hold in my heart hopes and dreams for them.

None of our six children had anything to say about who his or her parents and siblings would be. Each has taken what already existed and made the best of it. I certainly had adjustments to make before I was able to make the best of it. I grew up with one sister. She's enough older that I was raised almost like an only child, which is to say I had things pretty much my own way. As the father of six, I have seen some amazing changes in my personality, such as an increased tolerance of noise and a high degree of flexibility. The pertinent question, consequently, is not where we've come from, but how we're doing as a family—right now. Do we communicate well? Do we share our lives? Do we forgive each other? Do we encourage one another?

As a child, I went through a stage where I wondered if I were adopted. I imagine most children do. I was afraid to boldly come out and ask. So I searched for clues. After a time, I satisfied myself that I was not adopted. I suppose I needed a sense of belonging, of a secure place in this world of constant change. My concern was genuine. But what I really wanted to know was *not,* "Am I adopted?" but, "Am I loved and accepted?" Those are two distinct questions.

I want each of our six children to *know* that he or she belongs here. I don't want the "home-grown" varieties to linger on doubts like, "They didn't have any choice but to take me—the hospital would have kicked me out." True, we had some complex discussions trying to decide how to announce that Ellen was pregnant with child number six. We determined that the direct, head-held-high approach was best. Neither do I want our store-bought kids to ask, "If a parent gave me away once before, might it happen again?" No, it will not happen again. We are bound together legally. We share the same last name (no matter that it's strange). We are tied together by necessity—we need a roof over our heads, food in our tummies, and clothes over our skins. But something far more powerful and enduring is present in our relationship as a family. We are bound together by a gift from the Spirit—*love.* Yes, we sometimes get upset, cranky and impatient, and we say things we don't mean in a moment of anger. But we're a family. They're all ours and we're all theirs. And the whole bunch of us belongs to God. I can't think of anything else to say except, "Amen."

"... but ye have received the Spirit of adoption, whereby we cry, Abba, Father. The Spirit itself beareth witness with our spirit, that we are the children of God: and if children, then heirs..." (Rom. 8:15b-17a).

Nineteen

I THOUGHT TAXIS HAD METERS

I always thought taxis had meters, but cruising the streets of our city is an unmarked cab carrying riders hither and yon. And it has no meter. In fact, the passengers pay nothing for the service. The driver—me—picks up the tab and is expected to smile graciously about it. Neither rain, sleet, snow, nor an empty gas tank can deter the appointed rounds of our family limousine. A map of my routes would resemble a web spun by a crazed spider, crisscrossing the city in wild sweeps.

To prove to myself that there was purpose in my travels, I kept a log during one February. I noted time out and in, total miles, and any unusual events. I shall not reproduce here the entire document as its bulk approached that of an epic novel. One evening's journeys will give you a representative sample:

5:50—Left my dinner half-eaten to take Amy and her friends to the ice-skating rink.
6:05—Arrived at the church to pick up John who was working on the backdrop for a musical. I helped nail plywood.
6:25—Back home. "Don't take your coat off, Dad. I'm ready to go to Carrie's." Steve and I headed south. Her place was dark so he checked with a neighbor. Carrie, Steve's girlfriend, was waiting for him on the other side of town, five miles north.

6:45—Left "Romeo and Juliet" at the theater and turned home-
　　　ward.

6:57—Walked into the house to find Ellen rearranging the living
　　　room furniture. The hide-a-bed awaited my muscle power.
　　　I sat down and stared at the cold, soggy remains of my
　　　dinner.

7:50—To the ice rink again. Two of Amy's friends needed rides.

8:12—Home once more. I assumed I had two hours before
　　　retrieving Steve and Carrie. "By the way, Kel, we don't
　　　have enough milk for breakfast. And while you're out,
　　　would you stop by the drugstore, too?"
　　　"Sure, if I can buy myself a bottle of aspirin."
　　　"Oh, do you have a headache?"

8:30—Went shopping.

10:35—Steve asked if I'd take him and Carrie to Pizza Inn. "Why
　　　not? That's the only part of town I haven't yet seen to-
　　　night. What time shall I come back?"
　　　"Somewhere between 11:15 and 11:45, I suppose."
　　　"Could you be a bit more precise?"
　　　"Dad, I don't know how many people are ahead of us.
　　　Just show up at 11:15."
　　　"What if you aren't ready?"
　　　"You don't mind waiting, do you?"
　　　Yes, I mind, I thought. *I'd much rather be sound asleep
　　　by then.*

11:30—Arrived back at Pizza Inn. "Where've you been, Dad?
　　　We've been waiting forever."
　　　Good, I thought. *Maybe he'll appreciate how often I
　　　wait for him.*

Perhaps I shouldn't complain about providing a free taxi service. At least I know where the car is at all times. I do think, however, that I deserve to play the radio station of my choice. In spite
of what I want, the young person in the middle front seat instantly
and automatically starts poking the tuner buttons. "Stop grump-
ing, Dad, you get to sit by a window." True enough. I also get to sit
by the steering wheel, brake, accelerator and shift lever.

They have frequent discussions about who sits where. "Dad, John got to sit by the window all the way here. It's my turn on the trip back."

"She's right, John. You slide over and let Amy be there." John moves slower than slow motion. "Are all the doors locked? Has everybody gone to the bathroom?" I sound like an airline pilot making a preflight check.

Getting the entire family ready to go somewhere is organized chaos. Lost shoes must be found, tangles in hair combed out, and the family room "dog proofed" so Cindy won't chew toys and eat crayons. Getting everyone in the car makes me feel like one of those machines that crushes old automobile bodies. I push and cram them, hoping no one escapes.

One place I don't mind taxiing them to is the public library. They quietly wander through the stacks, then stagger out with a load of books. A little of the library's atmosphere apparently rubs off, because I'm rewarded with hours of peace and quiet.

As I drive about, every so often I lift my head high, thrust my jaw forward, and assert my identity. "I am not a glorified taxi service!" I proclaim.

A voice in the backseat replies, "Sure, Dad, we know. But could you drive a little faster? I'm going to be late."

"And let us not be weary in well doing: for in due season we shall reap, if we faint not. As we have therefore opportunity, let us do good unto all men, especially unto them who are of the household of faith" (Gal. 6:9,10).

Twenty

TRAIN UP A CHILD IN THE WAY HE SHOULD GO—HE'LL SOON BE BIGGER THAN YOU

"Train up a child in the way he should go," advised Solomon in the Old Testament, "and when he is old he will not depart from it" (Prov. 22:6, RSV). Solomon neglected to mention how old the child will be before this happens. I know it isn't sixteen. However, this is the age at which son John has grown taller than I. And he shows no sign of slowing down. Over the years, I have become accustomed to being the tallest in the family (when I stand straight, since Mom and I are almost the same height). I predict that in eight to ten years, I shall be one of the shortest family members.

I am falling behind in other areas, as well. Stephen (15) is probably stronger than I from his participation in athletics and his weight-lifting routine. Amy (13) can run faster than I. And all of them can whip me at checkers. Furthermore, they're learning things I've never mastered, such as the metric system and computer programming.

What's a humble father to do? My only hope is that we've trained them well in their formative years, because they all soon will be bigger, stronger, faster and more capable than I. I have the edge in experience, but what I consider to be my positive qualities, such as mature and mellow, they call old and tired.

We have tried to train them to respect others, especially their elders. We have attempted to teach them to esteem community leaders: government officials, doctors, pastors, police officers, and school administrators. While no leader is without fault, children (and adults) need to honor the position and the service rendered.

"I'm getting a D in algebra just because the teacher is lousy," a son righteously informed me.

"Wait a minute," I replied. "Did you turn in all your assignments when they were due?"

"Well, I maybe missed a couple."

"Did you ask for help when you didn't understand a concept?"

"Uh, not exactly."

"I rest my case, son. Whether you think the teacher is super, rotten, or so-so, you need to do your best. He's the one you're going to have for the rest of the term." If one of my kids has a genuine problem, I'll discuss it with the teacher. I will not, however, tolerate disrespect, which includes blaming the teacher for poor grades.

"Raising by praising" is the best method I know of "training up" children. Nothing else comes close. I've tried nagging, scolding and bribing. These simply aren't effective. Children don't respond positively and I always end up feeling guilty.

Report cards came home the other day. We were six for six: we had batted a thousand. They all received glowing praise. We do not reward their academic success with cash. We reward them by heaping on the praise and affirming their achievements. We'd like them to discover that the joy of learning is its own reward.

I find it easy to preach at kids, and not simply because I'm a pro. My classic opening statement for many fatherly sermonettes is, "When I was your age . . ." From their perspective, I was a child in the Dark Ages.

I believe in praising, not pushing;
in caring, not coercing;
in discussing, not dictating;
in motivating, not manipulating.

Occasionally, there are days when I feel confident they'll make it to productive adult life. They share willingly, act politely, and are thoughtful and compassionate. But the very next day, I despair. Their immaturity surfaces and they bicker over nothing, behave selfishly, and act plain silly. I shouldn't be surprised that they act like children; after all, they are. But I respond by not knowing whether to laugh, cry, or do both simultaneously.

Because of the pressures upon kids to be mediocre (at the least), and the urges to yield to destructive influences (at the worst), I fear for their bodies, minds and souls. Raising a family in the world today can be frightening. The news media readily spread the horror stories involving youth. We read of a boy who in anguish committed a violent crime against his family. We are given the staggering statistics (in bold type) of runaways, youth prostitution, and drug abuse. I fight back a sense of panic. I don't have all the answers. How can I ever know enough to be a competent parent? I don't even know how to warn them so they can accept my advice rather than rebel against it. I cannot be with them everywhere, all the time.

I want to trust the potential for growth that God has placed in each child. I want to allow our children freedom to explore the fascinating things in God's creation. I want them to see and touch the beauty in the world. I want them to find love and joy in their personal relationships. Yet I want to hold them close and protect them. "Who is that boy Amy walked home with from the school bus? Where does he live? Who are his parents? Why is his hair so long? Does he go to church? And if he does, is it on my list of 'acceptable' ones?"

You don't suppose that growing up is scary for them, too? I'll bet I look pretty old to them. Do they worry what might happen if I were to die? Do they fear that Mom and I may be contemplating a split? Are they distressed when I show concern about our inability to pay all the bills? And what kinds of intense pressure do they experience from peers at school and at play? It may be difficult to be good parents these days, but it's no cakewalk being a young person, either.

Perhaps we can derive security from the knowledge that we

parents and kids are all in the same boat. We're committed to one another "for better or for worse, for richer or for poorer." We know that the Spirit of God is guiding us through this wilderness, giving us power to keep going, and creating genuine hope in our hearts.

Not long ago, I realized a comforting fact: our six children are "training up" quite nicely. They're a long way from perfect, but they're good kids who are "in there plugging." Yes, they stay up past bedtime when Mom and I are out for the evening; they some-times procrastinate on their schoolwork; they get upset when they expect a yes and we say no; they hide vegetables under wadded-up napkins; they forget to turn off lights.

All factors considered, however, they're super people. There is a great deal of unhealthy activities they could be doing, but aren't. So I thank the Lord and keep training them up in my im-perfect, but loving way. I may also be in the market for elevator shoes.

"My son, if thou wilt receive my words, and hide my com-mandments with thee; so that thou incline thine ear unto wis-dom, and apply thine heart to understanding; yea, if thou criest after knowledge, and liftest up thy voice for understand-ing; if thou seekest her as silver, and searchest for her as for hid treasures; then shalt thou understand the fear of the Lord, and find the knowledge of God" (Prov. 2:1-5).

Twenty-one

IT'S A BEAUTIFUL GIFT—PS-S-S-T, WHAT IS IT?

I could tell he had worked hard to create it. The clay had a weary look from the repeated molding by small fingers, and the shape and contour were quite fascinating. It came wrapped in lined writing paper and taped with what must have been half a roll. "I made it just for you, Dad, for Father's Day." His eyes twinkled with excitement and anticipation as I struggled to unwrap the package. There it was. I smiled happily, offered my most sincere "Thank you," and gave him a hug.

"Do you like it? Really? Really?"

"Oh, yes, I think it's—it's beautiful." Then came the crisis; I couldn't figure out what it was. Maybe an ashtray, but I don't smoke. Maybe a vase, but someone had given Mom one for Mother's Day and it certainly didn't look like that. Maybe a wall plaque, but there was no hook on the back. Aha! A paperweight—it weighed a ton.

In case I was wrong, however, I decided to play it safe and consult my wife. But how? My son's pleasant, eager little face was still turned to me, trying to determine if I, in fact, appreciated his gift. He wanted to make sure I wasn't just being tactful to make him feel good. At this point, Mom came to my rescue. She saw the panic behind my grin. Turning sideways, she whispered in my ear, "It's a spoon holder."

"What's a spoon holder?" I mumbled through my mustache.

"You know, for the top of the stove."

"Oh·h·h." I profusely thanked our son for his special gift, for his creative efforts, and then added, "I'll put this on the stove right away. I broke the spoon holder Mom got when we were married, so this is exactly what I needed."

Everybody was satisfied. I had guessed correctly—okay, Mom did. Mothers are much better at such things. I think God gives them extra insight. I breathed a sigh of relief and gave Ellen a kiss of appreciation.

Being a father is demanding. I'm supposed to be strong enough to twist off stubborn pickle jar lids, rough enough to wrestle three kids at once, yet gentle and sensitive enough to soothe a child's hurt feelings. It's no wonder I sometimes apply the right quality at the inappropriate time.

Last Christmas we decided not to use any commercial decorations on our tree. There's hardly room for anything else with all the children's school and church originals, plus gifts from friends who are "artsy-craftsy." We appreciate the personal touch and the precious memories related to each item as we place it on the tree.

I managed to locate the Christmas boxes in our storage closet and brought them out, breaking neither anything within them nor any parts of my body. We unpacked the ornaments that had been carefully wrapped after last Christmas. "Remember this felt snowman Amy made in the fifth grade?"

"Oh, look at these Lifesaver dolls Grandma gave us." There are dainty macrame snowflakes and bright red bells knitted by a dear friend who died at a very young age. There's a bread-dough Santa that's so heavy it bends a limb almost to the floor. At the base of the tree we place the cardboard manger and plaster-of-Paris figurines (partially chewed by the first puppy we had). The tree is crowned with a bent silvery star we received the first Christmas after we were married.

As we decorated, Sara noticed the accumulation of store-bought balls still neatly packed in boxes. "Let's put these on the tree; they're so shiny!"

Mom quietly answered, "Honey, we're going to use only homemade ornaments this year."

"How come?"

"Because I like them better."

"Even ones made by little kids like me?"

"*Especially* the ones made by you."

"But what if we made mistakes and they turned out kind of—funny?"

"Dear, I like those best of all." Sara's expression betrayed a lack of understanding, so Mom explained. "I like homemade things better, not because they're perfect but because they're made with love."

Sara's face beamed. The corners of Mom's eyes moistened as she handed Sara a popsicle-stick angel. Sara balanced precariously, stretching to hang the angel as high on the tree as possible. I felt warm and joyful as I watched my little angel on tiptoe.

I expect to receive gifts on my birthday, at Christmas, and on Father's Day. On those occasions I'm alert and prepared to respond graciously to whatever they offer. Sometimes, however, they've surprised me. I've come home from a difficult day at the office, exhausted and famished, and fantasizing about steak with baked potatoes and sour cream. I walk in the door to the pungent smell of burnt oven. The girls have a "surprise" for Dad. They've cooked the evening meal all by themselves. The menu reads: crispy hotdogs, semi-thawed buns and soggy french fries. Lukewarm coffee is served with what I guess to be oatmeal cookies.

I could not remain disgruntled for long. Their radiant faces more than compensated for whatever the cuisine lacked. And the amazing fact is, I liked the meal. I didn't have to fake it. My taste buds were pleased and my stomach filled. In addition to preparing dinner, Amy and Sara cleared the table and loaded the dishwasher. I call that a complete treat.

Children do not always offer the most expensive or elegant gifts. Used bubble gum and combs with missing teeth will never make the pages of a Nieman-Marcus catalog. But they certainly leave a lifelong imprint in a dad's heart. Praise God for a child's desire to give! May I always be ready to freely receive, thus encouraging them to give and give again from the motive of love. And praise God for the intuitive powers of mothers!

"Whosoever shall receive one of such children in my name, receiveth me; and whosoever shall receive me, receiveth not me, but him that sent me" (Mark 9:37).

Twenty-two

WHAT THEY REALLY MEAN

We parents need the ability to interpret what children say. We can't always accept statements at face value; deeper, more subtle meanings are sprinkled into their youthful conversations. I'm not implying they don't tell the truth. But they do flavor their declarations to fit the taste of the listener.

Our children frequently preface requests with the phrase, "*But everybody else...*" "But everybody else: gets to stay up till midnight ... receives a bigger allowance ... has a car of his own ... always wears name-brand jeans." What they neglect to tell you is that "everybody else" is three friends whose parents are much more wealthy or permissive than we. There are four hundred other kids at the school who receive less allowance, go to bed at 9 p.m., wear plain pockets, and won't have a car until they can pay for it themselves (including gasoline and insurance costs). Parents must never assume a scientific survey has been conducted.

When work is to be done, a favorite ploy is to use the negative, "But nobody else has to: clean his room every week ... eat cooked vegetables before she gets dessert."

"Okay, guys," I reply, "give me a list of names. And while you're thinking, eat your string beans so we can have cake and ice cream."

There are other classic expressions. Allow me to offer my

translations of our children's most commonly used phrases.

"I can explain." They then make a gallant effort to list all extenuating circumstances. "The teacher lost my test paper . . .

"We had a substitute and I didn't know I was supposed to turn in my homework . . .

"The dogs were chasing each other, and they tripped me, and I fell over the chair, and the football popped out of my hands, and that's when the lamp got broken. It was the dogs' fault."

I have learned to read between the lines. I do trust the kids. But I know that explaining is an art form, a type of storytelling at which children are expert. I'm pretty good myself when Mom wants to know why I haven't mowed the lawn or put up storm windows.

"But Mom said . . ." This is offered when Mom is gone and cannot be reached for confirmation. The names "Mom" and "Dad" may be used interchangeably, depending on which is absent. It works best if a decision must be reached quickly. "Mom said I could go to the store, but it closes in fifteen minutes." What Mom actually said was, "You can buy more candy after you've eaten what you bought yesterday. You've had enough junk food." The child in question went directly to her room, devoured candy bars, gum and suckers, then reported ready to go as per instructions.

My stock answer to "But Mom said . . ." is, "In case you haven't noticed, I'm not Mom. I'm the one with a mustache." It helps if parents compare notes once in a while—every day. Because we talk to each other, I have a pretty good notion of what Ellen's likely to approve and what she's not.

"Couldn't you make an exception just once?" Translation: "If you're flexible on this issue, Dad, I've got you." One deviation implies open season on rule changes.

A similar expression is, *"You've always let me do that."* Two years ago I permitted them a special privilege, and they haven't stopped reminding me.

"It's not fair." The sibling in question was not afforded any favors, so had to be content with equal treatment. Often it has to do with the age difference. "Why does John get to stay up later than I

do? Maybe he's two years older, but I'm mature for my age. It's not fair." I reply that being fair has nothing to do with it. He might as well experience life's inequities in small doses amidst the comforts of home.

"Dad, I've learned my lesson." This is usually spoken prior to disciplinary action. So I reply, "I'm glad you have, son. Now, to make certain the lesson sticks and you retain the main points, I shall proceed with the punishment."

"Oh, Dad, you just don't understand." The reverse is probably true—I understand all too well. I know more than they think I do. When I was a child, I thought I got away with lots of sneaky things. When I became a parent, I learned differently. I can tell when they're up to something. They suddenly become eager to please after having been grouches all day. Or they may offer explanations for what happened before I even know a problem exists. They try too hard to act innocent.

"I wasn't anywhere near the refrigerator when the juice spilled." What bothers me isn't that they try to get away with things. I expect that. What bothers me is they imply I'm not bright enough to figure out what's going on.

"I promise if you'll let me _____ , I'll do _____ ." It's the old "Let's Make a Deal" routine. I often yield, particularly if they offer a creative approach! "If you'll let me stay overnight at Chris and Kelly's house, I'll go to bed on time for a month without complaining," or, "If you'll let me go to the movie, I'll clean my room as soon as I get back. I'll even clean the whole house!" The promise is often greater than their capacity to fulfill. But, of course, a modest pledge would have little dramatic effect.

"You never told me that before." They express this with shock, trying to convince me that I have never before uttered such a rule. I beg to differ. Every piece of advice has been repeated countless times. My most-used lament is, "How many times have I told you?" I now understand why God gave Moses the Ten Commandments on stone. There was no way they could be erased. When the Hebrews said, "Lord, you never told us that," He could reply, "Read the rock tablets."

"Times have changed, Dad." I agree, though I'm not certain

it's all for the better. And while times have changed, human nature hasn't. Kids try to play the same word games I tried when I was their age. What they don't know is that I'm as good (maybe even better) at it as they. I've had more years of practice.

"Yes, dear, I'll help you with the dishes in just a minute."

"The thing that hath been, it is that which shall be; and that which is done is that which shall be done: and there is no new thing under the sun" (Eccles. 1:9).

Twenty-three

POWER GOES FORTH

I now understand why beds should be made first thing each morning. It's not so the room will appear neat and tidy. The real reason is that unmade beds are too inviting; the lure of rumpled sheets is nearly irresistible. It's as though the covers grab my weary bones and pull me back in.

After all, it was a tough night; and today's my day off. I wander by the unkempt bed, glancing wistfully. *Ah, a few more minutes won't matter,* I think. *I deserve it. I could use the extra energy. This parenting business is exhausting.*

There often comes an insistent tugging on my pant leg. "Dad, I'm thirsty. Will you please get me a drink of water?" It's not that one small request is tiring. But the accumulation of such appeals adds up, until by evening I'm often worn out. It helps to remember that Jesus felt tugs, too. On one occasion, a woman who had been ill twelve years approached from behind and touched the hem of His robe. "And Jesus, perceiving in himself that power had gone forth from him, immediately turned about in the crowd, and said, 'Who touched my garments?'" (Mark 5:30, RSV).

As a parent, I experience the same outward flow of power. My children's daily needs, their tugs and pulls, their conflicts and joys, all cause an energy drain.

It requires much parental energy to support them at performances such as piano recitals and wrestling meets. It's hard work watching Amy or Sara sit at the grand piano, hoping her memory will function and her butterflies will subside. My stomach muscles tighten and my hands perspire. I utter a quick prayer asking for God's calming influence on my child in the spotlight.

Watching wrestling matches leaves me in a very weakened condition. When son Steve is on the mat and in danger of being pinned, I go through as many contortions as he in my attempts to help him escape.

Mental, emotional, and physical power goes forth from parents in the line of active duty. As children mature, they necessarily pass through stages of minor rebellion. My theory is that every child worth his salt has little streaks of rebellion. I don't mean he causes open conflicts or leads a mutiny. I refer to those instances when he asserts his individuality. Dad needs to be flexible and patient. The child isn't trying to overthrow parental authority. He's just testing his God-given talents to see how they work.

The family was assembling around the dinner table when Sara politely asked, "May I say grace tonight?"

"Of course you may, dear." Heads bowed and eyes were shut. A lengthy silence followed and eyeballs started to peek. Somebody snickered. "Hush!" I whispered. "You're going to pray, aren't you, Sara?" Another pause.

Her brothers fidgeted and one whispered through clenched teeth, "Hurry up, Sara, I'm starved."

"Um-m-m, dear God, I'm sorry it's taking so long. I'm just trying to remember everything I should tell You."

"Sara, you don't have to tell Him *everything*," Michael muttered. "He's God, so He already knows."

"Sh-h-h-h. Everybody quiet down, please."

"Dear God, thank You for such a pretty day. Thank You for hamburgers with catsup and tomato slices. Help my friend Kelly—she fell off her bicycle and scraped her elbow. Thank You for Mom and Dad, for Grandma and Grandpa, for my teacher, for—" I cannot verify it, but I think at this point in the prayer, Amy kicked Sara's leg. "Ouch! Stop it, Amy. Now where was I? Oh, yes—and thank You, God, for my brothers and even for my sister who makes me mad sometimes. Amen." I breathed a sigh of relief. Looking up, I noticed that David had eaten half of his hamburger. He must have been nibbling while the rest of us were quibbling. I pictured God about to fall off His throne in laughter from our escapade.

The Lord must receive special enjoyment listening to children's prayers. He may well grow weary of our so-called adult attempts to manipulate Him or wax eloquent. I imagine He appreciates the refreshingly honest expressions of children. For me, however, such a situation can be taxing.

I feel power go forth when the phone rings and it's one of them calling from school. He either needs something or forgot something. "You need *what?*" I grumble.

"We're having a party, Dad, and I was supposed to bring potato chips."

"Why didn't you tell me last night? I went to the store and could have bought a bag then. Now I'll have to make another trip."

"Sorry. I need it by second period."

"When's that?"

"In fifteen minutes, so hurry."

"I haven't shaved yet."

"That doesn't matter—but don't buy a bag of that cheap brand. Get something good."

"Beggars can't be choosers. Anyway, I don't have much cash. You'll have to be happy with what I can afford."

"So write a check. Amy's here, too. She wants to talk with you."

"Hi, Dad. I need a bottle of pop—a big one. We're having a celebration in social studies, and—"

"I know, you don't want a cheap kind. It's got to be Pepsi or Hires, right?"

"How'd you know? Bring it to the office as soon as you can. I've got to run, Dad. There are twenty other kids waiting to use the phone. Bye." I shaved as quickly as possible, dumped my piggy bank and robbed Mom's coin purse. Fifteen minutes later I stood in the junior high office, puffing, but holding chips and Pepsi.

Yes, the power goes forth continuously. That's as it's intended to be, because the power also comes in continuously. As rapidly as energy ebbs out, God's Spirit resupplies it. Countless times when I've been dead tired, a surge of God's power flows through me, and I'm ready again to play and work—especially play.

"And he said unto me, My grace is sufficient for thee: for my strength is made perfect in weakness. Most gladly therefore will I rather glory in my infirmities, that the power of Christ may rest upon me" (2 Cor. 12:9).

Twenty-four

THEY LOVE ME—WHISKERS, HAIRY LEGS AND ALL

Several winters ago, I decided to grow a beard. I'd had a mustache and sideburns for ten years, so why not connect all the fur? The children had other opinions.

"Dad, what's wrong with your face? You look grubby!"

"You're a pastor, Dad, not a bum. I'll be embarrassed when my friends see you."

The younger kids wrinkled their noses and curled their lips when I tried to kiss them good-night. "Ugh! You're not going to touch me, porcupine face!"

I persevered. As my whiskers lengthened and softened, they began to accept the new growth. "Dad, may I feel your beard?" Their first touches were tentative. Did they expect fleas to jump out or a fungus to attack their fingers? Eventually, I even received grudging compliments from our peach-fuzzed teenage sons. I think they were jealous of my ability to produce such lush facial hair.

My family has definite opinions of whether a beard enhances or detracts from my appearance. Yet whichever view prevails, they love me—whiskers, hairy legs, moles on my neck, rounded belly and all. And I love them—runny noses, untied shoelaces, dirty faces, sticky hands and all. I guess we deserve each other.

111

The father images portrayed by television often disturb me. There are two distinct and opposite types. First is the "know-it-all" dad with a sweet (though condescending) disposition. He is perpetually calm and eternally wise. He always has cash in his pocket, lives in a classy neighborhood, and drives an expensive car. It's a neat trick since he never visibly works outside or inside the home. He's just around. He has a freshly scrubbed, Ivy League look and is never unshaven on his day off. He manages the family's affairs from a favorite easy chair in the center of the living room. He never perspires, blows his nose, or has greasy hair. I think "Father Knows Best" was an excellent series, but I'm afraid it spawned this perfect father syndrome.

At the other end of the spectrum is the bungling, naive, incompetent dad, out of the Ozzie Nelson mold. Ozzie was a fine man, but he was a step behind, a dollar short, a day late. This type of television father is supposed to be humorous. Everything he tries he messes up. If his lovely wife doesn't correct him, the kids have to tell him what to do. He doesn't sit in the overstuffed chair; he's too busy frantically running hither and yon. Once in a while he's funny; usually he's just in the way, a lovable nuisance.

Neither stereotype is realistic or useful. The perfect dad is worshiped or adored from a distance. The frantic father is best ignored. I want to be both close to my kids *and* respected by them. I want the intimacy that allows them to see my warts and moles, but also my kindly blue eyes and genuine smile; to touch my bushy whiskers, yet to reach far more deeply to touch my heart. I want us to see beyond each other's superficialities to know the inner person, the one who cares, gets angry, is shy or lonely, asks forgiveness, or brings peace.

Fathers of our kids' friends pose another problem. I simply cannot compete with them and win. Diagonally across the street is the vice president of a junior college. If you were to compare his success and salary to mine—well, you can't because they don't. Directly across from us is a dad who was an all-stater. He can swish thirty-footers through the garage basketball hoop. A favorite uncle in town is a card shark, a marvel on roller skates, and a skilled pilot. Other dads drive racy sports cars, own vacation property on beautiful lakes, have had tryouts with major league teams, or wear elegant clothes and fancy hair styles. I can barely make lay-ups; I'm doing well if I skate around the rink once without falling down; I drive a humble little gas saver; and I have split ends.

The other day I descended into the pits of despair when a son informed me, "Grandpa is a lot more fun than you. He takes us fishing, lets us dig in his garden, and gives us candy whenever we want." Dull old Dad, on the other hand, reminds them to brush their teeth, wash their dirty hands, make their messy beds, and do other equally boring things.

I have decided, therefore, to accept my role as is. I am not Super Dad, able to leap piles of dirty clothes in a single bound, or to run faster than a speeding football pass. I'm a "dad-of-all-trades," able to do many things, though master of none. I'm the well-rounded, complete father, steady, dependable and on duty twenty-four hours a day.

I attempt to perform routine duties with grace. I have taught each child how to ride a bicycle, although several protested they would rather do it by themselves. I wonder what the neighbors thought as I scurried down the street beside a wobbling two-wheeler. My presence was for encouragement and for catching the kid before his or her tender knees scraped pavement.

I've spent hours upon hours throwing a baseball. "Keep your eyes on the ball—step forward with your left leg—snap your wrists when you swing the bat." I'm a veritable storehouse of baseball wisdom and the owner of a sore arm every spring.

I've shared carpentry skills with them—and shown them how to apply Band-Aids to the resulting nicks, scrapes and smashed thumbs.

Mom and I have shared the duty of cutting their meat at the dinner table from the time they had four teeth until they reached the age of seven or eight. I worry about adjusting to that inevitable moment when I'll have no one's meat to cut but my own. I not only cut meat, I'm the designated dumping station for food left on plates. Child number three doesn't like meat loaf, so I take hers to finish with my tossed salad. When they're all teenagers who eat everything on their plates (plus half of what's on mine, plus everything in the refrigerator), I'll lose weight. That's the reason I'm postponing my diet. I need to keep these extra pounds lest I waste away in the future.

I want to be the genuine article as a father: tough yet approachable; firm yet flexible; hardheaded yet sensitive. I want them to think I'm fiscally responsible but not a tightwad; morally upright but not a prude; spiritually deep but not self-righteously pious; wise in the ways of the world but not conceited.

They need me to be close and personal. I need it, too. Much of my time is spent being "at" them, encouraging them to do worthwhile endeavors. Often, I am "behind" them, pushing them to accomplish a goal. And I do so many things "for" them, I cannot possibly keep a record of my activities.

Important as it is for me to keep "at" them, nudge them from "behind," and to do "for" them what they cannot do themselves, it is my being "with" them that is of lasting, even eternal value.

My greatest gift is their greatest need: my presence, unmasked and unmixed. I offer what I have—whiskers, hairy legs and all. I do not need to compete with other dads or feel insecure from television images. I shall try just to be the best dad I'm capable of becoming.

So, bring on the razor blades, the beard has got to go. But the hairy legs stay.

"... for the Lord seeth not as man seeth; for man looketh on the outward appearance, but the Lord looketh on the heart" (1 Sam. 16:7c).

Twenty-five

THE MASTER OF MIGHTY PRONOUNCEMENTS

I cannot recall the specifics of time and place, or even which child was involved. I do vividly remember my inner turmoil and my patience being stretched thin to its snapping point like a rubber band. I turned up the volume on my voice. My eyes narrowed and a faint red tint crept up my neck toward my ears. I had an advanced case of anger.

I am a relatively calm person, but vulnerable to a few things. A sassy kid, as in that situation, was one, particularly if I was under pressure or tired. Since I was one or both, the fireworks went off. I shouted a mighty pronouncement of the tried-and-true variety (when upset, it's hard to be creative): "If you don't clean up this mess in two minutes, I'm going to ground you for twenty years!" Note how the punishment fit the crime.

"But, Dad, I'll be thirty years old, and probably married with kids of my own."

"Not if I don't unground you, you won't." I am by no means the reincarnation of Moses, the great lawgiver. I am, though, accomplished at issuing mighty pronouncements. Several years ago I had the habit of tacking to every decree the phrase, "Now I mean it!" When that didn't work, I would add a few more choice words: "This time I *really* mean it!" I eventually realized that if I had to say "I mean it," I had already lost. If they didn't perceive my authority initially, they weren't likely to be impressed with subsequent addenda.

"If I've told you once, I've told you a thousand times!" Sound familiar? Another useless utterance. Truth spoken with authority will be heard the first time. If it's but an idle threat, it will have little effect even if repeated. Truth can stand being retold; dumb is dumb forever.

My mighty pronouncements don't go in one ear and out the other. They seldom gain entrance at all. When I'm delivering one of my gems of wisdom, I wish they'd be honest and say, "Dad, I think that's the seventy-seventh time you've told me. Even if you repeat it a million times, I'm going to be stubborn and do it my way." That may sting my ego, but at least we now have a chance to talk about the matter.

For the most part, our children know how to handle me. John employs dry humor; he's a master at tongue-in-cheek. He often starts with grandiose schemes and whittles them down. "Dad, I need $25 for bowling this week," he pleads.

"You *what?*" I explode, not noticing his mischievous look.

"Well, I suppose I could manage with $10."

"John, it's usually only $3.50. Why the extra?"

"Oh, I thought I'd bowl a few additional lines, play some video games, and then have steak and fries." By now I see the twinkle in his eyes and the wry grin.

"All right, exactly how much do you need?"

"Four-fifty. We have to pay league secretarial fees." I gave him $5, feeling both generous and lucky to have escaped so cheaply.

Sara sweet-talks me while looking coy and batting her long lashes. "Oh, Daddy," she coos, "you're such a nice father. Do you think I might go to the little store? I'll hurry back. And Kelly's mom says it's fine for her to go with me." She makes it exceedingly difficult to say anything but yes.

David pulls the "I'm just a little kid" routine. "Dad, it's not fair. Just 'cause I'm the littlest, you never let me do anything."

Amy uses the written message. She leaves clever notes in unique places. I may open my razor case as I prepare for shaving and find a message inside. "Dear Dad, may I have Angie and Mindy stay overnight? Please, may I, a thousand times please? We won't be noisy. We'll go to bed on time. And I'll be good for the next hundred years. Your loving daughter, Amy."

Steve utilizes the comparison method. "Why can't I? You let John stay up till midnight last weekend." With five brothers and sisters, he has many examples from which to choose ammunition. He remembers with precision who got to do what and when.

Michael uses his considerable powers of reason. He lists all the positive factors to sway me to reply affirmatively. "It's a once-in-a-lifetime opportunity. The price is right and it's approved by a panel of dentists. So what do you say, Dad?"

"Okay, Mike, you may buy some bubble gum."

"It's good exercise for the jaw, makes my breath sweet, and it *must* be healthy because seven out of ten baseball players chew it."

"I said you may buy some, Mike."

"You did? In that case, may I have a candy bar, too? It's a source of quick energy, and—"

"No, son, only bubble gum. But nice try."

My pronouncements are usually words of caution. "Hey, slow down!" "Take it easy!" "Watch out!" Such phrases are foreign to their vocabularies. They instead demand with urgent messages. "When can I have it?" "I can't wait any longer." "I'll starve if you don't give me a snack right now." "When's dessert?" "I've simply got to have my allowance."

I try to meet them halfway. I speed up my response time and cut down on my mighty pronouncements. I ask them to go slowly on their demands and attune their hearing to my voice. It's a workable, though imperfect, system. Until a foolproof plan comes along, I shall seek to tame my urges to utter mighty pronouncements. They seldom seem to get anyone's attention anyway (except the dogs'). So I'll save my yelling for football games and for jumping into cold swimming pools.

"For thus saith the Lord God, the Holy One of Israel; in re-turning and rest shall ye be saved; in quietness and in confidence shall be your strength..." (Isa. 30:15).

Twenty-six

WHY DO I GET ALL THE DIRTY JOBS?

At the Judgment Day I will have a question to ask the Judge. I will not ask why good people suffer while stinkers seem to prosper; or why He didn't instantly solve the Middle East conflict. I will ask, "Why are there so many sticky, untidy things within reach of children?" Around our house we try to keep messy or breakable things out of the grasp of small hands. But God put dirt right on their level. It's inevitable that dirt and kids will get together because they share the same space.

On one occasion we were ready to go somewhere when I spotted dirty David (he was five). "David, look at you! You're an absolute mess! Go wash up and then change your shirt."

His eyes filled with innocence, he calmly replied, "Oh, Dad, it's okay. Kids and dirt belong together." He may have been right, but must they be constant companions?

The list of messy items is awesome: melted Fudgesicles, sticky bubble gum, runny school glue, squishy modeling clay, peanut butter and jelly, and chocolate-covered donuts. Mud may be an old-fashioned substance, but it's still one of the most effective for tracking across a freshly-mopped kitchen. Globs of grease adhere to little fingers before transferring to walls and windows. And have you tried to vacuum half a sandbox out of shag carpeting? I have toyed with the concept of an all-concrete house—no

need to vacuum, dust, or wipe. Just install faucets and periodically hose the place down.

Kids are creative about where and how they leave messes.
The girls drip fingernail polish on the floor and splatter makeup
on the bathroom mirror. The boys leave oily prints on doors after
they've worked on a bicycle or car. They also have a cute trick of
seeing how high they can jump. This would be a great exercise if
they didn't have to touch something at the apex. Even then, I
would not complain (at least not loudly) except that they never
jump and touch unless their hands are grimy. If you doubt the
truth of my observation, check out arches and ceilings in homes
where kids reside.

We set aside Saturday morning as cleaning day. Each family
member is assigned a task in addition to straightening his room.
Sometimes they work with vigor and enthusiasm, often with a
lack of both. The work does get finished, but we differ over what
constitutes clean. I define clean as the absence of dirt, the remov-
al of messes, and the eradication of everything sticky. They define
clean as the minor rearrangement of the same. The pile of dirty
clothes is moved from the middle of the floor to a corner of the
closet. Junk is crammed in dresser drawers (and they wonder
why the drawer won't close). Dirt is swept under beds. Sometimes
we let them get away with such practices. There comes a point,
however, when dirt cannot be hidden. There's just no more room
in which to stash it.

Speaking of accumulations, take a look (if you dare) in our
garage. We have eight persons who, if they can't find any other
place to hide junk, dump it in the garage. And shut the door. And
forget about it. Finally, Mom organizes a cleaning expedition for
the next Saturday. John is assigned the task of removing everything on wheels, which includes eleven bicycles, four tricycles,
three wagons, two lawnmowers, and one wheelbarrow (but no
partridge in a pear tree).

My jobs are to arrange the tool bench and remove any creepy
objects. The latter includes spiders, insects, rotting fruit that got
lost behind a box, and open paint cans with scum. I soon start hol-
lering at the kids for failing to put my tools back where they

belong. Then I recall who it was that left my saw buried in the woodpile and my electric drill bits mixed with the nails—me. With such a fine example, no wonder they neglect to put things in their proper places.

I'm told it's an honor to be asked to clean up the messiest of messes. Sure it is. Several Christmases ago, the children gave me a fancy plumber's helper, wrapped in bright paper and with a bow on the handle. Cute. I shouldn't brag, but my technique is quite good—excellent wrist action. I've had much practice.

I'm also the official yard patroller. It's the price one pays for owning two dogs.

I'm the self-appointed toaster cleaner as well. The last time I dumped the crumbs, I think there were enough to stuff a twenty-pound turkey.

In addition, Dad is insect exterminator. Our problem right now is ants. We have the best-fed ants in town. They receive a well-balanced diet of bread crusts, cookie crumbs, and cereal bits. Maybe they'll grow so fat they won't be able to squeeze through the baseboard cracks. An ant would be dumb to search for a picnic when a banquet is spread on our floor every day.

It requires constant vigilance to clean up after kids. I was helping compile a grocery list by taking a kitchen inventory. Inside the refrigerator I found a dried cheese sandwich hidden behind the egg carton, a half-eaten apple afflicted with brown spots, and a bowl of water with an orange tinge (someone had plundered the carrot sticks again). The bread drawer held two empty wrappers, sixteen plastic ties, five crusts, but not one slice of bread. The cupboard appeared to be well-stocked until I moved things around. Cereal boxes had nothing but a dusting of sugar coating; the saltine crackers were only crumbs at the bottom of the carton; the cookies were no more; and the potato chip bag rattled with a few lonely remains. In the freezer a tiny lump of ice cream clung desperately to the side of the carton. Of course, in the bathroom the toilet roll was stripped clean and the Band-Aid box contained only paper wrappings.

How do they do it? I seldom actually observe their forays. You can see vultures circling their prey and locusts swarming in dense clouds, but kids move stealthily.

I am slowly learning to accept these matters as integral parts of fatherhood. The only alternative is to be carted off to a home for distraught parents. We've tried to teach habits of neatness. But how can one fight innate tendencies such as rubbing hands along stairway walls? A child seemingly cannot go down stairs without dragging grimy hands on the wall from start to finish. If his arms are long enough, he gets both walls at once. If she's too short to accomplish that feat, she smears one side on the way down and catches the other on the trip back. Or vice-versa. The order matters little as long as both sides get equal smearing.

My unpleasant tasks also include those of being handyman and all-round-fixer-of-broken-objects. The kids have implicit faith in my ability to repair just about anything. In all humility, I must admit they're correct. With my soldering gun, tubes of Super Glue, and a variety of tape, wire, nails and caulking, I'm well-equipped. It's taken years to gather the necessary tools, but I'm ready for any emergency. Electronic toys are the trickiest, but I enjoy the challenge. If I'm successful, the look of joy on their worried faces is worth the blisters, scratches, and frustration it takes. My crowning achievement, without doubt, was using parts of five broken tricycles to create one of working order, and adding several coats of fire-engine red paint. It was more colorful and sturdy than most store-bought models, and still zips around the driveway.

I am flattered by being expected to clean up the worst messes and to fix the biggest tragedies. It can be a heavy responsibility, but I enjoy the role. I'm aware that somebody did the same for me as I grew up. I guess the difference between being a father and a child is not whether we leave messes behind. We both do, quite obviously. The difference is found in which of us has to clean them up.

". . . but whosoever will be great among you, shall be your minister: and whosoever of you will be the chiefest, shall be servant of all" (Mark 11:43b-44).

Twenty-seven

EIGHTH-GRADE MATH MAKES MY HEAD HURT

One of life's greatest challenges is trying to help a teenage son or daughter with homework. I enjoy being asked to assist from time to time, finding it a challenge to translate what I once learned into concepts they can grasp. It causes my intellect, as well as theirs, to grow as I adjust my dated methods to the new educational techniques. I was no slouch in my student days. As a matter of fact, I was class valedictorian—just don't inquire how many others graduated from that small rural school. I even took calculus in college, and passed, but it's none of your business what grade I earned. But enough is enough! Eighth-grade math makes my head hurt.

In case you've forgotten what junior high mathematics is like, here's a sample:

> Car A travels for three hours from point X. Car B starts at Y and drives for five hours. If Car A arrives at destination Z two hours before Car B, and if A goes 50 miles less than twice as far as B, what is B's rate of speed in kilometers per hour?

Who cares? With the price of gasoline, they both should have stayed home and read good books.

It's a real dilemma for me. I want to help, yet I have a horrible time determining the correct answers. But I get hooked and can't quit until I succeed. No eighth-grade math book is going to stump me! I usually arrive at the correct solutions, but there's a catch. "You're supposed to show your work, Dad. Teacher says so." I spent an hour and a half, guzzled three cups of black coffee, developed a sore scalp from scratching so hard, and endured Excedrin headache number seven to the third power. And I still have to show my work. It's a cruel world.

There are parental lessons to be learned from all this struggle, however. The first is to raise children who are smarter than their parents. It can be a humbling experience, but humility doesn't make my head spin like algebraic word problems do. James wrote, "God opposes the proud, but gives grace to the humble" (James 4:6b, RSV). Kids who know more than I do keep me humble and aware of my need for grace.

The second lesson is the importance of showing our work. I don't mean taking the kids to my place of employment, although an occasional visit may be helpful so they are able to visualize where I spend significant amounts of time. What I do mean is that parents should show their children the inner workings of heart, mind and soul.

Dad and Mom need to show their work in the area of family finances. I'm not suggesting we overload a child's capacity with more information than he or she can handle. I don't want my children to be anxious from wondering if we can afford this month's house payment, half expecting some Simon-Legree type to throw us out in the cold. Yet I believe it's helpful for them to know where we're plush or when the days in the month have exceeded the dollar supply in the checking account. Then they more graciously accept the strange casseroles we sometimes eat, and can better understand statements such as, "No, we can't go out to Arby's tonight."

In a family, it's especially important for Dad to show his work by expressing his feelings. I don't dump emotional burdens on them, but I let them know when I'm happy, disappointed or upset. They should see me cry in a time of sorrow. If I allow them to share in my ongoing emotional life rather than simply unload the finished product, I help them learn how to express their own feelings creatively. The *process* of being a family is more important than packaged results. Part of that process is conflict.

Ellen and I seldom have what might be called "fights," but we engage in some intense discussions once in a while. We also frequently ask for each other's forgiveness. It's healthy for the kids to see Mom and Dad work through minor conflicts to an adequate and peaceful resolution.

I also want to show my housework abilities. I think it's great for them to watch me do some of the menial tasks. I do not consider myself too high and mighty to help with loading the dishwasher, scrubbing the toilet, or folding clothes. It's honorable, necessary work. And the male can be as competent in performing them as the female.

A lot of things make my head hurt: political campaigns, seeking answers for an aching social problem of our age, the tangle of moral issues, and eighth-grade math. I shall continue my efforts to find solutions for them all. But it's demanding work. It's not easy to raise a family these days. It probably has never been. But I believe the emotional, financial and spiritual requirements are more intense now. I'm not fooling my children if I act as though being a parent is "a piece of cake" which demands nothing of me. I want them to know how hard I work and how fully I enjoy it.

God showed His work also. He wanted His people to know how much He loved them, He showed His work in a personal and concrete manner. He sent His Son. "And the Word became flesh and dwelt among us, full of grace and truth..." (John 1:14a, RSV).

Thus far I've managed to help three children through the eighth grade. That leaves three more to go. I hope we can make it. My fervent wish is that the school district won't change math texts until our youngest is safely in high school. By then I should have those word problems down pat.

Now, about seventh-grade English: diagramming sentences, underlining prepositional phrases, and listing subordinating conjunctions is not for me. There are some things the kids will have to do on their own. It's part of growing up.

"In all things showing thyself a pattern of good works: in doctrine showing uncorruptness, gravity, sincerity, sound speech, that cannot be condemned; that he that is of the contrary part may be ashamed, having no evil thing to say of you" (Titus 2:7-8).

Twenty-eight

IS THE WATER SUPPOSED TO BE GREEN?

When the youngest child, David, was about five, he was admiring our collections on the living room shelves. It's a wonder to behold. Hundreds of old purple and green bottles are semi-arranged, the most rare ones on the highest level. There are shells, rocks and sand dollars from vacations to the beach; antique books I've salvaged from New England bookstores; a jar with old-wheat pennies; encyclopedias we bought from a persuasive salesman when our first child was a baby; a clock with a pendulum; and assorted toys from Mom's and my childhood. What it lacks in artistic design, it more than compensates with variety.

In the midst of this aggregation sat a tropical fish tank, gurgling quietly. David pressed his nose against the cool glass as he watched tiny fish swim through the bridge and over the castle. Turning toward me, he asked with innocence, "Dad, is the water supposed to be green?"

I laughed. Mom laughed harder. "No, dear," I replied, "it's not supposed to be green. It should be clear. I haven't cleaned it for a while." Satisfied, he went back to checking the shelves. Later that same day, I cleaned the tank, scrubbing the accumulation of green from the sides. As I worked, I wondered why we had bought a fish tank and why we allowed animals to live with us at all.

We presently have two dogs, one cat, four pollywogs (one critically ill and swimming upside down), one tadpole transformed into a frog, and two tropical fish. We've previously hosted messy parakeets, nocturnal hamsters, and white rats who needed a home during school holidays. We've even assisted as the second grade's guinea pig gave birth to triplets and quadruplets.

Why us? What is it about animals that causes us to treat them so affectionately? Perhaps it's knowing we're needed. They're often cuddly and cute (tadpoles and white rats excepted). They depend on our care and feeding. They express gratitude by wagging tails, purring, chirping, or whatever they do best. And they never talk back.

But maybe the reason we let animals wander around in our home is more profound. Could it be a reminder of how precarious and precious life is? Most animals have relatively short life spans compared to us humans. Perhaps they encourage in us a reverence and respect for all living things.

So much for philosophizing. Whatever the rationale, ever since the invention of kids there have been pets. We're partial to dogs. Our first "child" was Eve, who as a pup received almost as much attention as our sixth baby, and did for a fact have more home movie footage.

Pets add a certain homey atmosphere. With two dogs, I get white hair on my dark blue pants and brown hair on my white sweater. Pets help teach responsibility. The question, however, is, to whom? Dad believes he's learned quite enough of that particular quality.

Thank the Lord, there are precious times which reward our efforts. Where, oh where, had that little dog gone? Max was only five months old. I couldn't find him anywhere, and I had searched every place a puppy could squeeze. Then I made another inspection of John's room. As I silently opened the door, a shaft of light spread across his bed. John was breathing deeply. I had noticed an extra lump in the bed earlier, but assumed it was dirty pajamas or the sheet all wadded up. (John is not noted for putting dirty clothes in the hamper or for neatly making his bed.) Was it my imagination, or did that lump move? I reached under the covers and pulled out a very warm, soft puppy. He didn't come willingly.

He probably sensed what was next: being dumped outdoors. For the remainder of the night there was an extra lump at the bottom of Mom's and my bed. We didn't have the heart to make him sleep on the cold garage floor.

I guess I'm a soft touch. Several years ago a young acquaintance called on a Friday, asking me to dispose of a cat. His mother had forbidden him to keep the creature, and since he couldn't bring himself to have the cat put to sleep, he asked if I'd do it. I wasn't exactly eager to comply, but his desperation made it impossible to say no. I picked up the animal and started driving home. Apparently, he'd never ridden in a car. He panicked, jumped on my shoulders, and dug his claws in—deeply. I made it home safely, found a large cardboard box, put him inside and securely closed the flaps.

I immediately called the animal shelter. "Oh, I'm so sorry," a very understanding voice responded, "we're just ready to close. And we won't be open tomorrow. Why don't you bring the cat next Tuesday?" Next Tuesday! This wasn't how I'd planned it. I rustled up some cat food, a dish for water, and an old blanket for a bed. I told the children that we were *not* going to keep this animal. After all, Steve was allergic to cat fur, and our dogs despised felines.

Word spread among the family, however, concerning the ultimate fate of Henry (they'd already named him). On the Monday evening before the trip to the animal shelter, all six kids marched up to the couch. I lowered my newspaper. "We've got it figured out," John solemnly announced. "We've pooled our piggy banks and have enough to buy a big bag of cat food. And if you'll help us, we'll build him a house. But we won't let you take him to the pound." Their looks were mixtures of hope and righteous indignation.

"Dad," Michael said, his hands stubbornly stuck on his hips, "we know what being put to sleep really means." What was a dad to do? I told the kids to put the money back in their banks; I wouldn't let our cat starve. "Dad, did you say *our* cat? Whoopee! We get to keep him!" We constructed a rather attractive home for Henry from plywood scraps, and insulated it with old cloth diapers. A sixty-watt light bulb provided heat.

I'm glad our children love animals. Nevertheless, I see no reason for our home to be a haven for lost and injured creatures. My valuable fishing worms were once nearly depleted by a sweet baby robin. It had fallen from the nest prior to its ability to fly. Henry took more than a passing interest, so the robin became a resident in our living room. I stretched chicken wire over a large box, scattered grass and bird gravel about, and added a tuna can for water. I also dug the worms. My garden had heaps of dirt everywhere from my searching. I could hardly believe how many it devoured. But what a fabulous conversation piece!

We took him (or her) outside for daily flying lessons. Somebody held Henry, who flexed his claws and drooled. The robin was gently nudged upward in hopes of discovering what wings were meant to do. We had little success. Why learn to fly when you can have all the juicy worms you want by standing in one place and saying "chirp-chirp"?

Well, I've got to stop writing and put a new light bulb in Henry's house. It's going to be cold tonight. And then I ought to clean the fish tank. It's got that slimy green look again. Maybe I should have told David that's how it's supposed to look. Honesty is always the best policy, though not necessarily less work.

"A righteous man regardeth the life of his beast..." (Prov. 12:10a).

Twenty-nine

YOU ALWAYS HURT THE ONES YOU LOVE

There's an old country-western tune with the intriguing title, "You Always Hurt the One You Love." I would add an "s" to "one," because I love several. I don't intend to hurt them. I feel bad as soon as I realize the pain I've inflicted. But I keep hurting the ones I love. I do many nice things for them: provide food and clothing, a warm house, and kiss them good-night. Then I slip. I say an unkind word. Those cross words sneak out too easily when I'm tired and cranky. Or in a moment of anger, I blurt out a sentence I wish I could grab and stuff back down my throat. I suspect we all have this problem.

I suppose I hurt the ones I love because they're available. We're stuck with each other and must take the bitter with the sweet, the irritating with the lovely. However, there is a distinct difference between honestly expressing emotions on the one hand, and hurting persons on the other. When I admit my feelings and openly accept theirs, we grow closer. If I put someone down or undermine his self-esteem, I destroy part of the trust we've built and thus damage our relationship.

That's when I feel guilty. Granted, I was weary and tense. But no mood, no matter how bad, justifies a verbal assault. I have observed parents verbally abuse a child, then moments later buy an expensive gift, attempting to assuage their guilt pangs. Such mistakes cannot be paid for; they can only be forgiven. The Scrip-

131

ture is very plain at this point. ". . . be kind to one another, tender-hearted, forgiving one another, as God in Christ forgave you" (Eph. 4:32, RSV). I've made numerous trips to my children's rooms to say, "I'm sorry."

I don't deliberately mess up, but I somehow get in the grasp of negative attitudes. I soon consent to the cycle of nagging, which goes something like this: They don't obey quickly enough to suit me, so I nag. So they start whining. So I raise my voice. So they look sad. So I feel guilty. So they act as if they got the better of me. So I nag all the more, caught in a vicious cycle. I nag. They sass. We all lose.

A better way? I prefer the "take and give" approach. We take each other just as we are and each give a little. For example, I try to tolerate their musical tastes, and they agree to turn down their tape decks a decibel or two; I listen for that telltale whine in my voice, and they try to avoid that squint-eyed glance in my direction. It doesn't always work, but it's certainly more effective than nagging.

Taking time to listen and to give clear instructions also helps. If they know what I expect and what the limits are, their average of success will improve. It also allows me to affirm them warmly and to act specifically when they err.

I hurt the ones I love when I fail to listen to their plans and dreams. Like a typical parent, I imagine what our children will be when they're grown. John will be a computer technician; Stephen, a professional athlete; Michael, a bank president; David, a minister like his dad and grandfather; Sara, a star basketball player in high school; and Amy, a cheerleader. I enjoy these thoughts, yet recognize what they are—fantasies. I hope to help them attain their own dreams and hopes rather than to inflict my expectations on them.

Sara says she wants to be a farmer. She tells me that kids at school laugh when she shares her idea. I doubt that she'll ever become a farmer once she learns of all the other career options, but I have never laughed about it. She has a genuine love of the earth and a reverence for plants and animals. I cherish the fact that she dreams and looks forward to being a productive person in society. I want to help open to her a world of hope and promise. I want her to gain confidence to reach her goals.

Kids have a marvelous capacity to dream. I was a world-class daydreamer as a teenager. Had I wasted time imagining myself a great concert violinist? Or a shifty halfback with the Forty-Niners? Or a captain of a great ocean liner? Not at all. By such dreaming I came to understand more clearly my unique gifts and abilities. Today I find myself engaged in an occupation that not only permits but actually demands the use of such imagination.

So dream on, Sara. Imagine yourself in all kinds of situations and places. I shall never say, "That's dumb; you couldn't do that in a million years." Instead, I want to say, "That's an interesting idea, Sara. Tell me more."

I can tell when I've hurt one of the children. John gets a pained, quizzical expression. Amy stamps her foot or slams her bedroom door. Stephen verbally defends his honor (he's a skilled arguer—maybe he'll become a famous trial lawyer someday). Sara's face reddens and tiny tears run down her cheek. I can feel Michael bristle within. And David offers a shy, sad smile.

The eyes of a child show what's transpiring in his soul. They gleam with joy, widen in amazement, sparkle with curiosity, and crinkle in the corners with laughter. A child's eyes have a purity because they are not yet dulled by mistrust and suspicion. A baby stares without blinking. When John was our only child, his intent gaze made me self-conscious. Then I realized that he was seeing me with purity, not guarding his sight. He was guileless toward those he saw. But now he's grown, and his eyes easily show hurt.

Yes, I sometimes hurt the ones I love. Often it's because I try to do too much for them. I want to protect them from pain, and therefore bind them too tightly, so I do too much *for* them and too little *with* them. I'm human, imperfect. But I'm what they've got for a father. So hang in there with me, kids. Keep those innocent eyes, those impractical dreams, and your willingness to forgive me, and forgive me, and forgive me.

"A new commandment I give unto you, That ye love one another; as I have loved you, that ye also love one another. By this shall all men know that ye are my disciples, if ye have love one to another" (John 14:34-35).

Thirty

WHY AM I SO PATIENT WITH OTHER PEOPLE'S KIDS?

When our children were babes in arms, I heard every noise they made in church. From my vantage point in the pulpit, I could detect their sucking on a pacifier in the last pew. No burp, whimper or cry escaped my notice. Of course, other parents brought small children to church also. Their toddlers might tear pages from a hymnal, play hide and seek under the benches, and grab a fistful of money out of the offering plate. I would just smile and continue leading the service. But let one of my kids scribble too loudly as he added artistic touches to the bulletin cover, and I'd immediately tense up. *Why doesn't she (their mother) do something?* I'd think. *Mrs. Van Winkle is sitting right behind them, frowning. She's easily upset, has no children, and is one of our most generous contributors.* These thoughts bounced around in my brain while my mouth kept on preaching.

If somebody else's child has a temper tantrum, complete with kicking and pounding on the floor, I hardly notice. If one of mine, however, swings his or her short legs and bumps the pew in front, I can recall the exact number of bumps. Perhaps I exaggerate. Yet the point is valid. I'm patient with other people's children but quick to note the faults of my own. I'm able to listen intently for an hour to a person I'm counseling, but at home I brush aside with irritation a son's or daughter's attempt to tell me what happened at school.

My patience with other people's children and my impatience with my own may result from an abundant awareness of the latter's imperfections. Other people's kids don't crunch carrots and apples like a starving horse, or eat soda crackers and leave a pile of salty white crumbs beneath the chair. Other people's kids don't scatter my newspaper to the far corners of the house—when mine finish dissecting it, restoration to its proper order is a human impossibility. "Okay, you guys, who took the front page? And why is the sports section cut to ribbons?"

A timid voice answers from the next room. "I'm sorry, Dad, but I needed an article to take to class tomorrow."

"That's fine," I reply. "Next time wait until I've finished reading it. You cut out the scores of the NBA and Stanley Cup playoffs, and your sister's junior high track meet."

I locate the front page on top of a stack of blocks in the family room. "Dad, that's our roof! Why do you need it when you've got all those other pages?" I return to the living room, find a section I've already perused and, when their attention is momentarily diverted, make a quick switch.

Yes, I'm acquainted with their failings, great and small. I know the precise disarray of their rooms without opening a door. I watch them pop huge wads of pink bubble gum all over their noses and chins. I observe them smash and scatter green peas on their dinner plates in the hopes we'll think they ate a few.

The truth of the matter, however, is that they know *my* trouble spots as well or better than I know theirs. They know my workbench is a worse disaster than all their rooms combined. They know that those black specks clinging to the bathroom sink are my whiskers; that those are Dad's muddy shoes in the entryway; that those are his dirty socks which missed the clothes basket. So it's a standoff.

Perhaps we focus too often on each other's imperfections and too seldom on the strong points. We need to see beyond the minor irritations to the deep joys. The God of redemption has given each of His children (even dads) redeeming qualities.

Maybe I'm less patient with my own children because I expect more from them. Parental pride makes me want people to think that I'm a good father, that Mom and I are not merely adequate, but superior parents. So I desire our kids to measure up, to perform well so we'll look good. I've spent considerable time dreaming about their futures, hoping and praying for them; and I've invested no small amount of energy and money in them. But God did not bring them into this family to make me look good, to bolster my ego, or to cater to my whims. He desires they be the best children they're capable of becoming (the Lord being their helper). I am called by God to assist in bringing them to maturity.

Patience is not achieved without lumps and scars. It is one of those prized qualities that can be learned only on the job. The Scripture tells us that patience is not an instant gift but a fruit which must grow and mature (Gal. 5:22). I advise caution when praying for patience. God is likely to give you the opportunity, such as three children simultaneously in diapers or a wandering son like our Michael.

Please understand, Michael was never a bad child, just extra inquisitive. He was the one who got lost in a Seattle department store; who wandered away at a crowded county fair; who got lonely and tried to find the school where his older brothers went.

He was three and a half years old, complete with rosy cheeks and unruly blond hair, when we moved to Wenatchee. The town is a slice out of middle-class America. The church I serve as pastor is rather conservative, though not staid. But nobody confuses our worship with a rock festival.

We'd been here only a few months. It was the formal 11:00 a.m. service. I was leading a congregational prayer from the lectern when I thought I saw a shock of blond hair bouncing up the side aisle. I couldn't see the rest of the body to which the hair was attached, but the cowlick looked familiar. I later discovered that Mike's mom and the church ushers were at this very moment frantically searching for the nursery escapee. If only they'd peeked into the sanctuary. Ah, well, it's now ancient history.

As I spoke the written prayer, I began my own silent petition. "Please, Lord, let that child belong to somebody else.

"Okay, Lord, I won't try to fool you. He's mine. Could you have mercy and send him back from whence he came?"

It was not to be. Michael boldly walked to the platform, approached the massive altar, stood on tiptoe, and attempted with all his might to blow out the candles. The candles were brand new, so the flaming wicks were at least four feet higher than his huffing and puffing. And such an effort could not be made quietly. If the congregation had kept their eyes focused on the printed prayer, they might have thought it was a second Pentecost, with the sound of a mighty rushing wind.

He puckered again and again. I said the "Amen" with a sigh of relief, rushed to the altar, and swept Michael into my arms. This was done gently, of course, for we were in front of God and several hundred witnesses, all of whom were snickering (God included). We made a hasty exit out the back door, found Mom and deposited Mike in her arms. "Would you try to keep better track of *your* son!" I huffed.

My next problem was how to re-enter the sanctuary unobtrusively. I considered crawling under the pews and hiding behind the oak pulpit. But the sopranos in the choir would have noticed. So I marched in as though nothing out of the ordinary had occurred. Maybe no one knew whose boy it was? Let me assure you, the few who didn't know soon found out. I pasted on a wan smile, frequently looked down at my Bible text, and endured the remainder of the service. Without exception, folks that day thought Michael's caper was a delightful diversion. And they were relieved he wasn't part of *their* family.

Had Michael belonged to someone else, I would have led the assembly in laughter. I admit it. I'm more patient with other people's kids. If mine would just stop testing my limits, I'd find it easier to be forbearing with them. In the meantime, however, I thank God for His unending patience with this imperfect father of six.

"I charge thee before God, and the Lord Jesus Christ, and the elect angels, that thou observe these things without preferring one before another, doing nothing by partiality" (1 Tim. 5:21).

Thirty-one

THE BATTERED FATHER SYNDROME

The role of father has become confused. Dad is caught in the crossfire between the high cost of supporting a family, the women's liberation movement, and the pressure of the male macho image. He is now expected to help more around the house, especially if his wife is employed outside the home. In the business of breadwinning, he must sometimes adjust to bringing home the smaller loaf.

It's not easy being a dad. It probably has never been easy. But in this age of mobility and changing expectations, there is left no universally accepted pattern to follow. It's hard enough being an effective parent in traditional terms, but having to be a pioneer, blazing trails into uncharted territory, adds to his anxiety and produces an emotionally battered father.

Dad faces the crisis of being the Great Provider. The list of what I am expected to supply is long and rapidly growing longer. The cost of rent or mortgage payments is astronomical. Designer jeans, ski jackets and Nike shoes swallow the dollars quickly. Mom went to J. C. Penney recently to outfit our children with personal items such as underwear and socks. The bill exceeded $100 without even breathing hard.

The cost of entertainment at home and in the community boggles my mind. I feel vaguely guilty if I can't provide as many

Atari cartridges as their friends have. I worry that I'm stifling their development when our budget precludes ski equipment and lessons. Schoolteachers are forever devising a project or extracurricular program that dips into our family's coffers; it may be only a couple of dollars, but one here and two there become significant. The kids no longer "nickel and dime" me to the poorhouse; I'm being dollared to death.

I'm in the bind of wanting to provide well for my family, yet sometimes not being able to do as much as I wish. Shall we slide a little deeper into hock? Shall Mom wear the same dress and Dad the same suit one more year? Will Montgomery Ward be satisfied with the minimum payment? The answer is "all of the above." If I'm not careful, I can easily play the martyr role—"Look at all I'm sacrificing for you guys; why don't you appreciate me more?" There's only one method of escape: refuse to play the Great-Provider game.

Mom and I must decide what the basics are and stop responding to every want. When we don't cater to a whim, we need to support each other so neither of us feels guilty for having said no. "But, Dad, everybody my age wears Calvin Kleins."

"Wrong, daughter. I know one girl who doesn't."

Our two older boys frequently inquire, "When are you going to buy us a car?"

I just smile and say, "Never. Cars are not included in your contract. You'll have to earn your own." I try very hard not to add "... like I did when I was your age."

I want to be an adequate provider. Attempting to be the Great Provider can do a back-alley battering on a father's ego. It's downright discouraging to know my paycheck is spent as soon as (if not before) it's in my hot hands. Sometimes when I get paid, I come home feeling on top of the world. I think, *We've got lots of money—look at our bank balance. Why don't we go out for a night on the town—dinner at a fashionable restaurant?* Then I enter the real world of finance through the front doors of the house. Daughter number one needs her flute repaired. Daughter number two fell, loosening a permanent tooth—she has a dental appointment in the morning. Son number three lost his new sweat shirt. (Why don't they ever lose old stuff that's ready for the rag bag?) Our eldest needs six dollars for a Spanish-class lunch at a fancy restaurant.

"Six dollars for lunch!" I shout. "You're going to a place I've never been because it's so expensive."

"Dad, it wasn't my idea. I'd have been happy to eat at Taco Bell."

My descent from the height of joy to the depth of despair is rapid. It gives me empathy for the father who stops at the local pub on payday. He wants to have the illusion of wealth, if only for a few fleeting moments. I don't approve of the practice but I know the feeling. The problem, however, is compounded because the bartender is quite willing to cash his check and relieve him of as many dollars as possible. Predictably, the poor bloke's spouse is none too pleased with either his expenditures or the company he's been keeping.

I receive a minor emotional battering whenever I see a media version of manhood. The image is of a tall, muscular, bronzed, blond-shocked man with two or more sexy women clinging to his body. It's usually in some exotic setting with white sand, crystal water, and absolute peace.

What happens when I take my short, semi-out-of-shape body home? Muddy cat paws speckle the hood of my car. Dandelions poke up conspicuously in our yard. A neighbor's dog has feasted (none too neatly) on our garbage. My wife is up to her elbows in spaghetti sauce and mozzarella cheese, and she does not instantly kneel before my male presence in wide-eyed admiration. She just turns her face toward me so I can peck her cheek with a polite kiss. I have to fight for a section of the evening paper, and I end up with the society page, complete with wedding announcements and Dear Abby.

Dads formerly got respect simply because of their title and its prestige. That's ancient history. The role is no longer held in awe. Once upon a time everything a father said or did was considered correct unless proven otherwise. These days my every utterance is questioned. It's up to me to defend my position. I earn every bit of respect I manage to corner. I don't care what they call me; they can call me Dad, they can call me Father, or they can call me Pop—as long as they say it with love and respect.

I admit there are times I need some friendly battering. When I act the tyrant or the spoiled little boy, I ought to be given a swift boot. When I neglect to show affection for Mom, I deserve a sharp jab in my side. Most of the time, though, I need warmth and acceptance because we fathers are human, too.

I've developed a few techniques to heal my battered psyche. I often use "panic prayer." This is the type where I yell, "Help me, God!" He understands even if I don't spell out the details—there usually isn't time to elaborate.

Going to church helps, at least if the hymns aren't too lively. Worship consists of praise and of receiving God's eternal Word. But it also serves as a breather between rounds before the bell rings again.

The ability to laugh is indispensable. The kids conned me into playing a video game where chunks of rock crash toward my space ship. I was to fire missiles to disintegrate the rocks before they smashed me to bits. I flopped—but I hadn't laughed so hard in months. I became hysterical attempting to guide my tiny ship through the huge asteroids. The healing properties of laughter proved far more important than earning a high score.

One of my best traits is my balance of toughness and tenderness. I get battered every so often, but I keep coming back for more. I vow never to become callous or hard of heart. So, on with the fracas.

"These things I have spoken unto you, that in me ye might have peace. In the world ye shall have tribulation: but be of good cheer; I have overcome the world" (John 16:33).

Thirty-two

RELAXATION AND PRIVACY ARE ENDANGERED SPECIES

I'm stretched out on the carpet, drifting and dozing to the mellow sounds of FM music. I rouse sufficiently to say, "Ellen, dear, wake me when it's time for bed." That doesn't make sense (but show me in the fatherhood manual where it states all of life makes sense). I ought to climb into bed, snuggle under the covers, and sleep without interruption. Agreed. Yet I seem to need a transition between life in the fast lane and the complete stop of bedtime. So I collapse on the carpet to relax and unwind. The real reason I don't retire to the bedroom is the chance there may be a delicious snack tucked in the refrigerator: roast beef, cheese, mashed potatoes, squash, lettuce salad. I make a great sandwich from leftovers (if it's in the refrigerator, I incorporate it into a sandwich).

Dad and Mom need times of relaxation, moments of privacy to find refreshment for body and soul. If such occasions are not possible, exhaustion is around the corner, which may result in our succumbing to irritability, despair or illness. Jesus taught His disciples of the need to retreat periodically from the crowd and be renewed by the Spirit. His advice is equally true for parents. Once in a while, we must go apart from immediate demands and pressures, else we will come apart at the seams.

I'm perfecting the art of relaxing on the run. In our home, there are few lengthy periods of uninterrupted time. If I'm going to relax, I've got to use those bits and pieces, such as the half hour between the last child's departure for school and my arrival at the office. It's a short but precious time. I savor my last cup of coffee; or use the bathroom without fear of intrusion (being so daring as to leave the door open); or do absolutely nothing, staring out the window at the distant hills, guessing what the weather will be from morning's prelude of clouds, wind and sun. I admit I'm some-times late for work. But I don't punch a time clock. I can sneak in the back way and act as though I've been in my office since 5 a.m. Nobody believes me, but I avoid excessive guilt feelings that way.

I can relax while waiting for a traffic light to change from red to green. Please don't honk at me. I probably need rest more than you need to hurry to your next destination.

Sitting in front of the wood stove, while a fire cheerfully crackles and dances, brings inner comfort. A short walk in the or-chard has the same effect, as does reading my favorite sports magazine or the humor sections of *Reader's Digest.*

I don't even let the time spent rinsing the dinner dishes pass unused. It's an effective moment for relaxation because no one else risks coming close. They're all afraid of being asked to help, so they evaporate outdoors or to their rooms, to television, or if there are absolutely no other options, to schoolwork. I stand at the sink, mesmerized by running water, whistling a merry tune, alone with my thoughts and messy plates. It's a small price to pay for a moment's peace.

I recently had a birthday. Somebody tried to tell me it was number forty-something. I find that hard to believe and/or accept. It seems so short a while since I was a fuzzy-cheeked high-school youth. How time flies when I'm having fun! It indeed goes rapidly when I'm doing significant work and enjoying my family. So what did my wife and kids give me for the occasion? A pipe and slip-pers? A magnifying glass? Geritol? Or a footstool? None of the above. They bought me a weight set and bench. I have a vague impression they were hinting about my physical condition.

We spent the evening arguing with the instruction booklet.

When all was properly assembled, family members tried the leg lift, did a few arm curls, and bench pressed as much as they could. I was inspired. I came home from late meetings, donned my gym shorts, and pumped plastic (my weight set isn't made of iron). Arnold what's-his-name won't get much competition from my physique. I can't see much change in the mirror, but I can certainly feel something happening. These sore muscles had better pay off with firmness. If a little pumping and puffing will improve my health and tone up my body, I'm all for it.

I usually collapse after a workout at home. I can't do that, however, in the big world where image is important. When the parents play against the kids in a practice soccer game, I have to keep going and act energetic even though my legs feel like rubber and my lungs are wheezing. I admit that my muscles are arranged differently than they were twenty years ago. The problem is, my male pride is still in place and demanding attention. For a father whose work is basically sitting or standing in one place, exercise in moderate doses is relaxing. It's a refreshing change of pace for one whose most vigorous activity is pounding on the pulpit.

I also find it relaxing to play games with the kids. Hide-and-seek is good because when I'm "it," I can take as long as I wish counting to one hundred. They begin to wonder if I've gone to sleep—"seventy-seven, seventy-eight, seventy-nine, z-z-z-z-z." Cowboy-type games are pleasant, since I can cleverly manage to be shot, tomahawked, or otherwise "done in" early in the game, enabling me to lie on the ground and rest.

Three summers ago, we installed an above-ground swimming pool. We weren't able that year to have an actual vacation, so we splurged on a pool. We dug in the hard clay soil to level a twenty-one-foot circle, carrying dirt away in a wheelbarrow, an old blue wagon with squeaky wheels, and a tiny plastic wagon. We made quite a parade as we carted load after load down the street to deposit on an empty lot. The owner of the field appreciated our filling a low spot in one corner. We wrestled with the metal sides and struggled mightily with the vinyl liner. After much trial and error, we determined which hose and clamp went where. The magic moment arrived. Everyone gathered around while I switched on the pump. It whirred into action as water swished through the filter. "Yippee! We did it!"

We anticipated a refreshing summer immersed in our new pool. During the installation, we had sweltered in 100-degree temperatures. No sooner had we finished work, though, than abnormally cool weather settled in the Wenatchee Valley. But a few goose bumps and shivers didn't deter us. The next summer was properly hot. We lumbered to the pool like hippos to the deep spots in a river. I now understand why those behemoths lie submerged with only snouts and eyeballs protruding. That is the ultimate in relaxation.

Privacy is a rare commodity, an endangered species in most families. I don't protest crowding around the dinner table as long as I have room to operate my left hand, since that's the one I use to shovel in food. I also accept being crammed inside our little blue Fiat. It's cute, though not designed to accommodate a family of eight. But I draw the line when it comes to the bathroom.

When lathering up in the shower after having carefully locked the door, I grow anxious if I hear footsteps approach. The doorknob rattles and I yell, "Somebody's in here!" As the lock is skillfully picked and the door swings open, I pray that whichever child it is doesn't have half the neighborhood standing there wide-eyed.

"Oh, I didn't know you were in here, Dad!" he or she exclaims with genuine surprise.

"You thought maybe the door locked itself?" I sputter. Can't a man be left alone for just a few minutes?

I realize that we need times together to touch and be touched, to hold and be held, to snuggle, cuddle, give hugs and squeeze hands. It feels good to have a warm child crawl between Mom and me in the early morning. Jesus drew the children close to Him, gathering them in His arms to bless them (Matt. 19:13-15). We are therefore fortunate to have a family room where we watch television, play games, assemble jigsaw puzzles, enjoy our fireplace, and just lounge or hang out.

We are also privileged that each person has the possibility of privacy. Stephen's sanctuary is his room. He shuts the door, turns on his tape deck, and is alone with his thoughts, dreams and feelings. John finds his special moments later in the evening—he's a night person. He retires to his room with a book, and our two dogs for companionship, and reads into the late hours.

Mom has the utility room. Not very exciting, perhaps, but it's all hers. Amid the freezer, shelves of canned fruit, and the ironing board, she has her desk. It's usually piled high with end-of-the-month bills and the kids' school papers.

Amy and Sara retreat to their respective rooms, finding joy in dolls, posters, frilly curtains and colorful bedspreads. Mike and David head downstairs to their shared room to play with an impressive Star Wars collection. Their room's clutter adds to the sense of privacy—no one else can find a way safely through the mess.

My spot is right here, pounding away on my ancient Royal typewriter. I made the maple desk in high-school woodshop. It's solid, though not precisely square. This is where I create and express, muse and meditate. Here I experience frustration when words balk. Here I exult when ideas flow through my fingers onto paper.

Our family has places and occasions of togetherness. But each of us has a special little corner as well. We thank God for both togetherness and privacy, and we pray for wisdom to know when we need which one.

"... *commune with your own heart upon your bed, and be still*" (Ps. 4:4b).

Thirty-three

WHY DON'T THEY EVER ASK EASY QUESTIONS?

Sometimes it's exasperating. Sometimes it's exhilarating. I'm referring to conversations with a small child. Once, when David was four years old, he swaggered up, looked me in the belt buckle, and said, "I'm as strong as you, Dad."

"Well, Dave, I'll bet you're pretty strong, but it'll be a few years before you're as strong as I am."

"Yeah, you're a whole lot bigger than me. But are you as strong as God?"

"No, son, I'm not. Only God is as strong as God."

"Right," David added with conviction. "He's got the power!"

He's also got all the answers, and sometimes I feel as if He forgot to tell me what they are. That doesn't stop children from asking the questions, however. Youngest son, David, has been the worst of the lot. He wasn't much older than two when he asked, "Where'd you guys get me?" Whenever children ask a particularly hard or potentially embarrassing question, they seem to turn their high-pitched voices to full volume. Not receiving an immediate reply, he said, "Hey, I asked a question. Where did you get me? At K-Mart?" It was a serious matter for him. Mom turned away, covered her mouth, and quietly convulsed with stifled laughter.

"No, dear, we didn't get you at K-Mart," she said. "God gave you to us." She paused, hoping his inquisitive mind would take a different tack. His blue eyes twinkled as he replied, "Great! That's 'cause He knew you needed me." Having solved that specific problem, he toddled away looking quite satisfied. Mom hurried to her sewing room, relieved for the moment, to gather her thoughts in case he returned for a second round.

Children are not intentionally difficult (at least not usually). They just want answers to big questions. They assume big people have the correct replies. The problem is that adults have often quit asking and searching. We are led to believe that learning ceases when the diploma is received; that truth is an elusive quality forever beyond our grasp. So we retreat to the safe and comfortable answers, those with objective certainty. But the big questions won't go away. Kids just keep asking.

Michael's middle name is Winston, after Ellen's only brother. Winston was the eldest in her family and would have inherited the weekly newspaper Grandpa and Grandma labored forty years to build. Tragically, he was shot down and killed in Austria during World War II. We've occasionally discussed what happened and have looked at the medals he won. Sure enough, somebody (somebody being Sara) asked, "Why are there wars, Dad?" If I knew that I'd win the Nobel peace prize.

"Sara, it's hard to say. Maybe it's because people don't talk enough to one another. Perhaps we don't ask honest questions like you do. And people who don't know each other very well find it easier to be unkind. What do you think?" (It's sometimes effective to answer their questions with another question, until they get wise.)

"I asked you first, Dad." (Okay, it didn't work this time.)

"Well, honey, I don't know any good reasons—at least none that explains all the destruction and pain. People and nations start fighting and can't seem to figure out how to stop."

"You mean like when Amy and I argue and won't quit?"

"Exactly, except in a war, folks don't just yell, they kill."

Speaking of names, about once a month one of our children is likely to inquire where we got his. With the length of our last name, we tried to keep first names short and simple. I remember how tough it was in grade school to spell my name—sixteen letters in all. Every time we moved and I switched schools, I'd have to pronounce and spell it over and over. The only thing I dreaded more was that someone might find out what my middle name was. At my present stage of life, I use a shortened form of my first name and pretend I don't have a middle one. I hustle people past my diplomas and professional credentials before they have a chance to read my full name.

Since our children will have to live with their names, they're entitled to some sort of explanation. All six have middle names taken from one branch or the other of our family tree. We were quite conservative in our selections, omitting names like Tennessee Ellen and Marcus Leviticus. The last two children received Mom's and Dad's first names: Sara Ellen and David Kelvin. It has to do with roots and heritage and bearing the family standard into the future.

Kids ask tough questions needing forthright replies. What's an abortion? Why do good people get cancer? Why are so many children in the world hungry and homeless?

With the relatively large number of divorces today, children from stable homes start wondering about their parents' marriage, especially if a close friend has suffered separation from one parent or the other. One of ours hesitantly asked, "Dad, are you and Mom planning to get—uh-h-h—a divorce?" I reply as honestly as I know how.

"Michael, no one plans to get divorced. Sometimes problems happen which seemingly can't be solved. Sometimes husbands and wives say so many hurtful things that healing their marriage becomes very difficult. But don't worry. Mom and I are not going to get divorced. Though we may yell at each other once in a while, we really are in love. I can't guarantee we won't have problems, but I do promise we'll always try to work things out." I gave him a longer answer than was necessary—it's a common trait of preachers. It seemed to calm him, however, and he settled into the big chair, curled his legs over the arm, and finished reading his book.

So go ahead, children and youth, put Dad on the spot. Keep asking those hard questions and raising those complex issues.

May I never give cheap or shallow answers to your profound searching.

"And all that heard [Jesus] were astonished at his understanding and answers" (Luke 2:47).

Thirty-four

"ARE WE THERE YET, DAD?"

The summer of 1981 was adventure time for our family. We had planned a trip to the East Coast because we wanted our children not only to read about this country but to experience its size, beauty, and history. The thought of traveling 7,000 miles in a six-passenger station wagon (12 years old and growing tired) momentarily cooled my enthusiasm. In addition to the eight of us, we also would need to carry sleeping bags, suitcases, food boxes, and favorite toys.

Mom's wisdom came to the rescue. "Why don't we rent a motor home? There'd be room for the kids to move around." In other words, they'd be out of Dad's way while he drove. We presumed there'd be a substantial savings by avoiding motels. Worse than the cost, however, is the look from the motel owner when I inform him we're a party of eight. I never know whether it's disapproval because of his concern for overpopulation, or anxiety over the possibility of an eight-person wrecking crew.

So Ellen and I went shopping for a motor home. Commercial renters asked too much for too little. We despaired until we checked the want ads. Behold! A couple in town listed a twenty-five-footer at a reasonable price. We hustled over to make arrangements. It sat in the driveway, shiny and impressive. I wondered if I'd be able to manuever something that large through rush-hour traffic in New York City.

It was not accidental that we contracted for the motor home during school hours when none of our children was present. And we were purposely vague concerning the exact size of our family, referring to them as "the children." We felt it better to inform the couple gradually of what was in store for their vehicle. They proved to be gracious in all our dealings.

We wrote to friends in New England, my sister in Connecticut, and our congressman in Washington, D.C., to warn them of our impending visit. They all responded warmly, the congressman motivated by my reminder that in a few years we'd have eight votes to cast.

We secured a house-sitter for the three weeks we'd be gone. This was more out of concern for our dogs than the house. They're lovable nuisances, and we couldn't stand the thought of them languishing in a kennel. We hired Brenda, a recent high-school graduate, to feed Max and Cindy and scratch behind their ears.

Mom made lists—dozens of them! If we had more moms, with their incredible list-making abilities, in government positions, this nation would soon be well-ordered.

Stephen wanted to pack half his worldly possessions. "Son," I informed him, "if you take that much, there won't be room for our necessities. You'll have to cut down."

"These are necessities," he replied immediately. "What do you expect me to do the whole way, stare at the yellow line?"

"Well, I thought perhaps we'd sight-see—you know, look at fantastic landscapes and historic places." I received a look of disdain.

"Dad, I've seen it all on television." His pronouncement confirmed the rationale for our trip: to have a firsthand experience of this great nation.

Neighbors came out to see us off. The one next door seemed almost too eager to wish us bon voyage. I don't blame her for looking forward to three weeks of tranquillity.

Day one served as a shakedown cruise. We went only 150 miles to one of Ellen's sisters. I began to get the feel of our home on wheels. Our children settled into their appointed places with the usual territorial disputes. "Dad, John's touching me."

"John, please move over and give Amy room."

"I have. And anyway, I didn't touch her. She bumped me."

"I did not! You stuck out your elbow." Conversations while traveling with children can be both stimulating and frustrating.

We stopped at one of the cleanest service stations I had ever seen. I didn't cringe or shudder when I walked into the men's room. While the two huge fuel tanks were being filled, everybody was instructed to use the facilities. We were barely back on the highway when I heard a voice from the rear call, "I've got to go to the bathroom."

"That's not possible," I muttered.

"A lot you know, Dad. I really do."

"Why didn't you go while we were stopped?"

"I couldn't. There wasn't enough time."

"There most certainly was!"

"Not after I found my gumball. It fell out of the machine and rolled under the counter. It took me a long time to find it."

"Is that what you're chewing?"

"Of course."

"Can you hold on for a while longer?" I inquired.

"I don't think so, Dad. I've really got to go." It's difficult to make good time when stopping every twenty-five miles for potty breaks, snacks, and other real or imagined emergencies.

We alternated days of sight-seeing with days of long mileage. We spent a day of leisure in Yellowstone Park, followed by a six-teen-hour, 550-mile jaunt to the Black Hills of South Dakota. About forty-five minutes after pulling away from the Yellowstone campground, a daughter chirped the familiar refrain, "Are we there yet, Dad?"

"No, we have 515 miles to go."

"How long will it take us? Will we make it before the swimming pool closes? And what about the video game room?"

"If all goes well, we might make it. But we got a late start this morning."

"It wasn't my fault," one of them protested. "David wouldn't get out of the bathroom."

"I couldn't 'cause I was stuck. I didn't know how to unlock the door, so don't blame me."

We ate breakfast and lunch in the motor home, which saved both money and time. On our first big splurge, we stopped at a classy restaurant where food isn't prepared before you arrive. The kids weren't accustomed to waiting while our meal was being cooked. A waitress actually visited our table, brought glasses of water, and served food on china. We thought it advisable for our children to experience this old-fashioned method before Styrofoam takes over completely.

As we left, Sara said, "Hey, Dad, you forgot your money. It's sure lucky I saw it beside your plate."

"Huh? Oh, thanks. That was a tip for our waitress."

"What's a tip?"

"It's a way of thanking her for being so helpful."

"Why don't you just shake her hand and say 'thanks'?"

"Yeah, Dad," an older brother added. "If you're going to leave money lying around, give it to me. I could use it for video games tonight."

By the time we reached Washington, D.C., we were ready to spread out. Togetherness is wonderful; however, 3,000 miles had caused it to wilt around the edges. In the foyer of the Smithsonian Institution's National Museum of Natural History, togetherness came to a screeching halt. After dagger-like looks, threats of walking home (to Washington State no less), and a few tears, we resolved the tension quite nicely. Mom devised a buddy system for the remainder of our Smithsonian visit. Oldest and youngest sons went off hand in hand. The girls skipped merrily away together. And the two middle boys (whose interests were compatible) headed another direction. Mom and I sat down and went nowhere. We didn't care if the wisdom of the ages was housed here; we wanted to catch our breath, rest our weary legs and survive.

It was a special vacation. We shall always remember the summer of '81. On our return trip, we grew a bit impatient in North Dakota. No offense to the fine folk who call that home. We were just anxious to be home, see how the dogs were doing, check the garden, tell our friends about our adventure, and go to the local video room to demonstrate newfound skills.

"Behold, how good and how pleasant it is for brethren to dwell together in unity" (Ps. 133:1).

Thirty-five

PUTTING AWAY THE CRIB FOR THE LAST TIME

The used crib had been a cherished gift. We received it while students, and a notch above poverty. We had dreamed of a crib with natural finish, but this had a thick crust of white paint. I bought cans of paint remover and retired to the basement to scrape. Each wooden slat required much elbow grease. I completed the project a few days before John arrived.

It had served us well through five more babies. Tiny tooth marks now dotted the bars. The connecting bolts had loosened from one child's constant rocking and another's attempts to climb in and out (mostly out).

When Amy joined our family, Ellen decided the varnished hardwood needed a coat of pink—something to do with matching a pink-and-white dresser. It required three coats. The next child was a boy, so pink surrendered to green. Then came Sara (pink again), and finally David (green trim).

After all the coats of paint, several mattresses, and various foam bumpers, it was time to unbolt the crib and put it permanently into storage. Youngest son, David, was ready for a big bed. We were pleased. David was excited but anxious. "What if I fall out? There aren't any sides, you know."

I wasn't prepared for the feelings which surfaced within me. I suddenly realized there would be no more diaper pail, no more pacifiers, no more crib, and no more babies. A twinge of regret

158

swept through me. Our whole life for nearly ten years had revolved around infant care. I was having to accept one of the passages of a normal, healthy family.

I look forward eagerly to what lies ahead. But it's not easy to lay aside the joys and even the struggles of the past. Five years later, I still become nostalgic when I open the storeroom and see the crib gathering dust.

Putting away the crib for the last time is not the only adjustment Dad and Mom must make. Our children have grown from slippery babies in the bathtub to modest young persons who take long showers. The change occurred almost imperceptibly. Sara (nine years old) was ready for her bath one day when she noticed it was the same water in which two brothers had bathed. (When kids aren't very dirty, we recycle water.) But this day she turned up her button nose and huffed, "You don't expect me to use 'boy' water, do you?"

"Water is water," I replied.

"Not after boys have been in it," she retorted. Though I was in a hurry to complete everybody's bath, I pulled the plug, cleaned the tub, and refilled it with "girl" water. That was the start of the transition to showers.

Showers at our place are not two-minute quickies. The kids like the long, drawn-out variety, where the mirror becomes fogged. Then they can scrawl messages and draw pictures on it. I appreciate clean kids. I do not appreciate large electric bills. "How much longer are you going to stay in there?" I ask, while visions of the wildly spinning electric meter dance in my head.

The telephone is another source of adjustment. Once upon a time, it rang for me. No more. I still get to answer it, but seldom does the caller want to talk with me. "Yes, John's here. I'll see if I can find him."

Convenient though it is, the telephone can be a source of conflict, especially if the family has only one line. "Steve, you've been on the phone for a half hour," I whisper. "Your time's up. I'm expecting an important call."

"I'm almost finished, Dad." That means he'll hang up anywhere from three to thirty minutes later.

I know the day is coming when once again all calls will be for Mom or me. Strange as it may seem, I think I'll miss the battle of the telephone.

Parenting produces a bundle of mixed emotions. Amy had come home from school and gone directly to bed. Normally a "go-go" girl, such behavior meant she was sick. Both Ellen and I had commitments that evening; however, with a sick child, one of us needed to stay home. I was elected because I wanted to catch up on some reading. After the kids were tucked in bed, I settled into a soft chair with a book on the grief process. I had just completed a passage about the tragic death of a young person when I heard loud coughing coming from Amy's room. I tiptoed beside her bed, watched her breathe for a few moments, and gently touched her small body. Only then was I able to return and concentrate on my book.

I trust God with all my being. Yet, I sometimes worry about our children's health and safety. I need frequent reassurance that He is "...close beside me, guarding, guiding all the way" (Ps. 23:4b, TLB).

Talk about ambiguous feelings! When David walked out the door for his first day of school, I was a jumble of pride and anxiety. *What a fine looking lad!* I thought. *But why did he have to grow up so fast?*

I'm sure he will do well. But what if he loses his lunch money? Or what if he needs to use the bathroom and can't find where it is?

He's so handsome in his new shoes, fresh haircut, and stiff jeans. He's off to face the world. But he's not very big—barely above my waist. There's so much he yet has to learn. Will he find anybody to play with at recess? Will his teacher realize how clever he really is? Will he find his way back home after school? The noise of his presence had sometimes been irritating. The hush of his absence was agony.

Managing mixed emotions is part of being a parent. Praise God for feelings, even though we often must expend considerable energy untwisting them. Life without joys and sorrows is no life at all.

We plan to keep the crib until grandchildren come along, and then the cycle will begin again. I hope the first one is a grandson. That way, I won't have to change the color. There are already so many coats of paint, I'm sure there's another can of remover in my future.

"To every thing there is a season, and a time to every purpose under the heaven: ... a time to weep, and a time to laugh; a time to mourn, and a time to dance..." (Eccles. 3:1, 4).

Thirty-six

THE FAMILY IS GREATER THAN THE SUM OF ITS PARTS

I like to putter around the kitchen. It's a change of pace from my usual activities, and besides, I delight in sampling my creations. Cakes from scratch are my favorites. Sometimes the results are rather unique, with a specific gravity approaching that of lead. But the family is brave and ventures a nibble. Thankfully, my cooking usually tastes much better than it looks.

A cake is more than the ingredients which were mixed and baked. A wonderful reaction occurs, a working together that brings forth an appetizing product. Each ingredient is essential, yet in the blending and baking each is significantly changed. So it is with a family. Mix us together under a common roof; let us work, play, eat, argue and cuddle, and something greater is built. One dad, one mom, plus six children does not equal eight. It equals a family. We are more than a mere collection of individuals; we are a special unit deserving even the label "sacred."

The family is greater than the sum of its parts. My moods and quirks aren't what determine our family's life, although I'm an important cog in the mechanism. Who would dispose of spiders if they didn't have me handy? My individual abilities and needs, however, are not what ordain our style and direction. The beauty of family life is that my individuality is enhanced by making cer-

162

tain our family comes first. Rather than try to conform them to my ways, I seek to use my peculiarities in a manner that enriches us all. We rub off on each other because we're close. Once in a while the rubbing produces friction, but the blessings help me endure this by-product.

John was our first child. It wasn't fair, yet we had to practice on somebody. He was a fairly strong-willed boy. He'd wobble over to the TV set and twist every knob his chubby one-year-old fingers could reach. We tried sweet reasonableness. "Now, now, Johnny, please don't do that. It isn't good for the television." His fingers just twiddled all the faster.

We attempted to divert his attention. "Here, son, play with these blocks. Aren't they wonderful?" While Daddy built a tower, Johnny resumed turning the dials. It's both amazing and frightening how fast such short legs can travel. Next we moved the TV higher, not yet having witnessed the prodigious climbing abilities children possess. We finally resorted to spanking his soft little hand.

We persevered with many late-night consultations and deep sighs. The problem was finally solved, though not by our parental wisdom. He outgrew it. We survived because something greater was at work in our relationships, something we wanted to last. Something greater than a temporary conflict between parent and child was present, keeping us loving and patient.

When the Pharisees had criticized Jesus for plucking grain on the Sabbath, part of His reply was, "I tell you, something greater than the temple is here" (Matt. 12:6, RSV). That "something greater" can be present in our families; it is nothing less than the Spirit of Jesus, the living God.

There's a pronounced difference between *having* children and *being* a family. People frequently ask, "How many children do you have?" I reply that we have six. I ought to say that we *are* a family with six children. We *have* a house needing a coat of paint; we *have* two cars in need of being washed; we *have* a bank account in need of funds.

We *are* a family. We belong to one another, bound by ties of a shared heritage, loyalty and love. We do not possess each other. If

I think I *have* someone, I'm likely to view his role as fulfilling my needs.

One dreary morning Mom and I were nestled in bed at 6:45, when Amy burst in waving an elastic belt. Amy is an early riser. Her body awakens totally and instantaneously. My body wakes up in stages—first my eyes open, then my mouth functions, and eventually my legs move. There she stood at the foot of our bed. "Dad, I thought I told you to fix this. I have to wear it today." It was not a propitious time to ask, nor did she use the desired tone of voice. I had been reveling in the warm covers, carefully avoiding all thoughts of duty and responsibility.

Amy is still learning that our family is greater than the immediate gratification of her needs. It will require more lessons for her, and for all of us. (Some days I feel that my kids' concept of a father is akin to a vending machine, programmed to respond to the command, "Hey, Dad, gimme!" I do become perturbed at such moments, but I try to avoid a bitter attitude.) So I asserted myself. I explained to Amy that she was most welcome to snuggle in our cozy bed before 7:00, but she was never to issue an ultimatum prior to 7:01. She got the message. And I fixed her belt after breakfast.

Just as important as how they treat me is how I treat them. Sometimes I behave as though they're small persons with no emotions or decision-making capabilities, who have no choice but to fall in line because I'm the biggest and earn the money. My authority should not be used to line them up but to build them up. All it takes to line folks up is a crack of the whip. To build maturity in others requires liberal doses of time and patience. It's worth the effort, however, since the family is greater by far than all my money, tears, sweat and chewed fingernails. (Actually, I don't chew my fingernails; I bite on the adjacent skin.)

We are more than what you see at first glance. We belong to an extended family (do we ever!). Mom is the youngest of six daughters of an old-time central Washington family. Her sisters and their families have scattered, but we keep track of one another. When her family gathers, what joy there is! And what noise and confusion! We all talk too much, brag more than is necessary, and over-overeat. It's great for the whole clan to assemble. It's also a relief to return to the relative simplicity and peace of our own home. Except, what do we do when they hold it at our house? I guess we learn with Amy that the family is greater than our own needs.

One method of emphasizing the importance of a family is record-keeping. Mom is our official recorder and statistician. She has a baby book for each child, complete with a hand print, a lock of hair, and a bathtub photo. Our genealogy is listed along with a chart of their height and weight. These baby books are well-loved and oft-used. It's good for Mom and Dad to thumb through and recall that our awkward thirteen-year-old with a cracking voice was, such a short time ago, a double-chinned infant who made cooing sounds, needed his diapers changed, and wanted to be held in a lap and rocked.

Mom pastes news clippings in scrapbooks and annually sorts through the imposing pile of school materials. We just about need a separate room for keepsakes, mementos, photo albums and home movies.

I've postponed mention of movies because—well, because there's nothing else quite like them. We received an inexpensive 8 mm camera for a wedding present. We filmed my graduation from college, our trip to theological school in Boston, and have hundreds of feet of New England's magnificent fall foliage. And then, of course, we filmed our kids.

I'm the producer, director and cinematographer. We have lots of reels from John's and Steve's early years and a few less for Amy. The last three kids seldom got top billing; we were either too busy or too poor, so they were featured only at birthdays, Halloween, Christmas, Easter and summer vacations. Two or three times a year, we have a family movie night. We get lots of requests, such as: "Dad, show the one where I'm hanging from the roof." "Dad, remember when I was learning to ride a bike and kept falling down?" (The law of equal time comes into effect here.) "How come Mike got to see two of his birthday parties and I only got to see one of mine?"

Replays of significant family events strengthen our bonds,

and induce positive feelings and peals of laughter. We become aware of how much growth and change has taken place. We become aware that we each are part of something bigger than ourselves; that we each are part of a living, growing family. Our family is not just a machine with several moving parts. It is not just an organization whose members all live under the same roof. It is not just an institution for raising, guiding and educating children. It is *a family*: two people God brought together to share the rest of their lives, and the children whom God gave them the responsibility to raise up to adulthood. And we all must live for each other, helping the other to become a person he never could have been if he hadn't been in our family. Separately, we are eight people standing on sixteen legs. Together, we are a family. and much more than the sum of its parts.

"Two are better than one; because they have a good reward for their labor. For if they fall, the one will lift up his fellow: but woe to him that is alone when he falleth; for he hath not another to help him up. Again, if two lie together, then they have heat: but how can one be warm alone? And if one prevail against him, two shall withstand him; and a threefold cord is not quickly broken" (Eccles. 4:9-12).

Thirty-seven

FOR EVERYTHING THERE IS A SEASON

We bought an Atari for Christmas. With it we can play seemingly every game ever devised: golf, baseball, chess, blackjack, auto racing, soccer, etc. We even can engage in tank battles and World War I dogfights. The Atari joined a multitude of electronic games and calculators in our household. Now when I was their age (oh-oh, here it comes), there were no such marvels.

This new toy has caused me to wonder how I passed the time when I was a child. I must have sat in a corner and twiddled my thumbs. But I recall being active. I listened to the radio (to great shows, such as "Big John and Sparky"), read dozens of books, and went to Saturday matinees. With no Walkman, if I wanted music outdoors, I had to whistle or hum. I had no battery-operated walkie-talkie, just two tin cans connected by a length of twine. I used the front porch of our house as a battleship under fire, a stagecoach pursued by desperadoes, a castle surrounded by evil knights, or whatever else my imagination conceived. Maybe I wasn't destitute after all. I learned to create my own entertainment rather than passively wait for someone else to provide it.

Times have changed dramatically and I feel rather incapable, so I try my best on the Atari. I sneak into the family room, after the kids are tucked into bed, and practice. I learn more easily when there are no beady eyes peering over my shoulder and no guffaws ringing in my ears. The pros in our family can play these games, chew gum, carry on a conversation, and read a comic book, all at the same time. Since I spent my formative years in relative sim-plicity, I probably shall never be on their competitive level.

But there are times when I feel competent as a parent. I must be doing something right because they're healthy and strong kids. Their latest dental check-up revealed only two cavities in six mouths. They're earning decent grades. And they all go to church with us. Three of the six really enjoy it; two have a good time once they get there; and one can hardly wait until the benediction is pronounced. Those are fairly good percentages. Knowing that the Lord has a sense of humor, it will probably be this last one He calls into the ordained ministry.

There's a time to hold them, squeeze them in my arms, and cuddle them on my lap. There's also a time when I need to push them out the door; a time when I must wait and watch, agonizing as I imagine all the terrible things that might happen.

There are times when I gather the whole family under my wings, experiencing fellowship and unity. There are times when I send them off alone, to spend time dreaming and reflecting.

There's a time to work hard and a time to play hard. Our rec-reational favorites are playing tag in the front yard and hide-and-seek in the orchard, throwing a Frisbee until it lodges on the roof, riding bicycles, and playing "hot box." This latter game is similar to what happens when a base runner is trapped between bases as his opponents attempt to tag him out. It's especially exciting when two dogs join the fray.

There's a time to be serious, and a time to be silly; a time to notice every detail of their activities, and a time to ignore all but the loudest crashes. There's a time to arm wrestle and smile; a time to arm wrestle and frown; and a time to quit arm wrestling altogether.

Family life has seasons. Ours is in early summer, if I calculate correctly. The children are well-grounded and growing rapidly. No longer do Mom and Dad have to attend to their every need. I re-call the joy when our youngest one learned to dress himself and tie his own shoelaces. Now they do favors for us, such as bringing

breakfast to our bed. It takes all the willpower we possess to calmly remain under the covers while hearing the incredible noises in
the kitchen. But we wait, knowing there has never yet been a
mess we couldn't clean. In the winter of Mom's and my life, there
may come a time when we'll need them to attend to our every
need. If so, the cycle will have been completed.

For everything there's a season. When they were babies, we
strapped them in an infant seat, placed them between us and off
we'd drive. I am presently relegated to the middle with my legs
pretzeled over the drive shaft hump. John sits behind the wheel.
Though he took driver education at school, he asked me to give
him additional lessons. My legs were never so sore as they were
after our first session. I don't know how many times I stamped a
nonexistent brake pedal. It's a wonder I didn't push my foot
through the floor board. In spite of my help, he's become an accomplished driver.

When I look back, the seasons seem to have moved by quickly. It was just a short while ago that I walked the floor with Michael
on my shoulder, that the diaper pail smelled up the entire house,
that I was an expert at warming a bottle, and that Amy sucked her
thumb.

I can still visualize Grandma rocking steadily with a baby
across her knees, rubbing its back to relieve colic. No one had a
better technique than she. That season is forever gone, and I remember it with fondness.

May I appreciate the joys and work of this present moment,
knowing that it, too, will soon slip into the past to join the ranks of
our family history.

*"The days of our years are threescore years and ten; and if
by reason of strength they be fourscore years, yet is their
strength labor and sorrow; for it is soon cut off, and we fly
away. . . . So teach us to number our days, that we may apply
our hearts unto wisdom"* (Ps. 90:10, 12).

Thirty-eight

A DAD'S PRAYER OF THANKSGIVING

Lord,
I give You thanks for my family.
In the hustle and rush
of each day's demands
I don't often say it to You
or to them.

Thank You, Lord,
for jeans with holes in the knees
and for sneakers with a kid's toe sticking out,
for broken shoestrings
and coat sleeves that hang
six inches above the child's wrist,
for bathtub rings
worthy of the *Guinness Book of World Records,*
and for doorknobs so sticky
I nearly have to pry my fingers loose.
I'm truly thankful
because they mean our children are
active,
healthy,
able to run and slide,
dig and climb.

171

They're busy
growing,
stretching
and moving.

Thank You, Lord,
for a kitchen counter full
of dirty dishes,
for a magnificent assortment
of crumbs scattered on the floor,
for an oven
that sometimes huffs and puffs
but cooks just as effectively
as a sparkling, silent, new one.
I'm thankful
because we have an abundance of food.
It may not always
be exactly what my taste buds crave
but all of us are well-nourished.
It's better to have food in our stomachs
with dirty dishes in the sink
than a tidy kitchen
and children with hunger pangs.

Thank You, Lord,
for the noise of youngsters at play,
for the sound of a trombone lesson being practiced,
for shouts of joy when a game is won
and the loud moans when a game is lost;
for their inability to sit still
at the dinner table,
in church,
or at any other place.
I'm thankful
for their energy and vitality,
their imagination and creativity.

Thank You, Lord,

for the simple joys of being a dad,
for the gleam in their innocent eyes,
for bunches of dandelions
clutched in stubby hands,
for hugs around my legs,
for cookies still warm from the oven
with chocolate chips
ready to melt in my mouth;
for moments when I'm lying on the floor
with one child perched on my chest,
another's head nestled on my belly
and a dog curled at my feet.

Thank You, Lord,
for renewing my energy
after the girls have had a slumber party;
for making the money last
till the end of the month.
I can't figure out
how You do it, Lord,
when we have a loan payment and a repair bill
for the station wagon,
medical insurance premiums and our doctor's statement,
a big water bill—
and kids who don't look any cleaner.

Thank You, Lord,
for children's forgiving hearts.
I mess up so often as their father,
forgetting promises (which they always remember)
or speaking in a spirit of irritation,
not because they deserve it,
but simply because I'm tired.
I deeply appreciate how You
and they
give me second chances.

Thank You, Lord,

for active grandparents
whose patience is helped
by knowing they can send their grandchildren home,
who give the appearance
of having all the time in the world,
whose pride is not based on accomplishments
of their progeny,
and who possess the fastest picture folders ever kept
in purse or billfold.

Thank You, Lord,
for sinks and soap,
showers and tubs,
dishwashers and washing machines,
brooms and vacuums—
for all manner of things that fight dirt;
for moments to catch my breath,
for Your restoring of a parent's frayed nerves,
for times when my kids and I communicate,
though we speak not a word.

I'm sitting in our family room
this evening
basking in thankfulness.
The free-standing fireplace spreads its cheer.
I'm glad it works so well,
considering all the effort required to install it.
I'm feeling weary
and a bit financially strapped (as usual).
There's an awareness
I'm not as young and frisky as I once was.
But it feels very good
to be a father.

Amy and Sara
are tucked in their double bed upstairs
reading books from the school library.
Their blue-checkered bedspread is pulled tightly

under their cute chins.
They snuggle side by side
finding comfort
and courage
from each other in the approaching nightfall.

David and Michael are lumps
in their twin beds downstairs.
They usually push the beds together
to create a huge one
with a crease down the middle.
A high-intensity lamp
sends a narrow beacon of light toward them
as Michael softly reads to David.
The room seems filled
with wide eyes,
peace
and brotherly love.
Cinnamon-furred Cindy lies
at the foot of their bed,
the picture of relaxation
with her doggy paws extended and floppy ears askew.

Stephen's radio
is quietly playing a lullaby
of rock music (if that's not a contradiction of terms).
John is sprawled in his room
as only a teenager—
whose legs have grown faster than his coordination—could,
reading science fiction.

The television set is silent—
a miracle
of no small proportions.
The house feels secure,
solid,
safe.

Tomorrow, Lord,
when the hassles resume
right where they left off,
when the make-it-through-the-day marathon
begins again,
may I remember
how thankful I feel right now.
Help me to say to the kids,
"I'm happy I'm your dad."
They don't automatically know
how much I appreciate them
and how proud I am to be their father.

Lord,
I am most thankful
that You've seen fit to stick by me.
I've made so many mistakes as a parent,
You'd be more than justified
in relieving me of my duties.
But You've stayed by my side
constantly.
Can I do any less with them?

Yes,
this earthly father
appreciates the continual help
You offer
as the Heavenly Father.
I couldn't handle the job without
regular infusions of Your divine power,
large doses of Your supernatural wisdom
and loads of patience from on high.
Thanks again, Lord.
Amen.